Out of Body Experiences

BY **GENE SCHMITZ**

WITH CHANNELED COMMENTARY AND EXPLANATIONS THROUGH

ROBERT SHAPIRO

LIGHT Technology PUBLISHING

ISBN-10: 1-891824-95-3
ISBN-13: 978-1-891824-95-1

Published and printed in the United States of America by:

Light Technology Publishing

PO Box 3540
Flagstaff, AZ 86003
1-800-450-0985
www.lighttechnology.com

Out of Body Experiences

BY GENE SCHMITZ

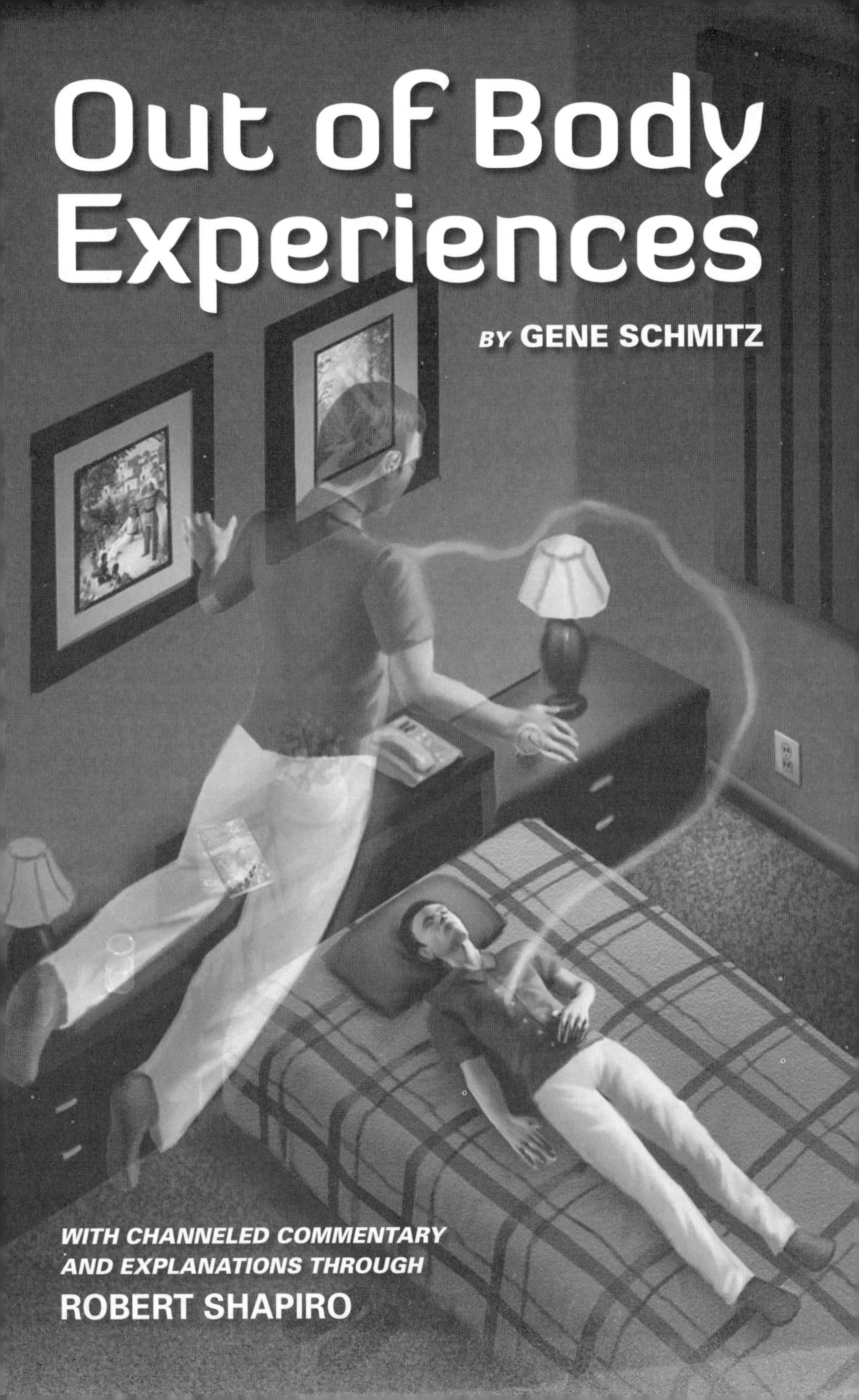

WITH CHANNELED COMMENTARY AND EXPLANATIONS THROUGH

ROBERT SHAPIRO

CONTENTS

Introduction

For the past forty years, I have spent much time in the spirit world while leaving my body behind. I did not ask for these experiences and I certainly did not want them, at least at first. They were so different that I was truly terrified by them for some time. It took a number of years for me to accept these experiences as something good because they were totally at odds with my Catholic upbringing and religious beliefs.

I am over sixty now, and after considering how much work and effort that several beings from the other side have exerted to show me the many adventures our souls can look forward to in a world beyond the physical, I feel that I need to share my story.

—Gene Schmitz

Part One

Out-Of-Body Experiences

by Gene Schmitz

CHAPTER ONE

Early Childhood Memories

I was born September 27, 1941, in the same farmhouse where my father and my grandfather were both born, five miles southwest of the small Western Oklahoma town of Thomas. This area lies in the middle of America's heartland—an area often called the Bible Belt. I am the oldest of four children, as was my father. My father's family is German Catholic and predominately a farm family. My mother was the oldest of seven children. She was born into a Baptist family about twenty-five miles west of Thomas. Her mother's father was a preacher.

When I was three years old, my family—which now included Ronnie, a younger brother—moved to Springfield, Missouri, when my dad took a job with a large farm machinery company there. I remember the apartment house where we lived and the big building where my dad worked. After a couple of years, we moved back to the farm in Western Oklahoma. My memories of our short stay in Missouri are all pleasant except for the long, hot, dusty trips in the back seat of a 1941 Oldsmobile coupe before auto air conditioning was around.

When we moved back to Oklahoma, we lived with my Grandpa Carl, Grandma Genevieve, and my daddy's youngest brother Joe, who had not married yet and was still living at home. The first several years of my young life were spent learning farm chores, such as feeding and caring for the many farm animals and learning to milk cows by hand. The farm work started at sunrise and continued until dark, six days a

Here I am a young boy, about to head off on my paper route.

week. Sundays were spent attending Mass at the small Blessed Sacrament Catholic Church in town.

I soon started school in nearby Custer City at the age of five. The first day was quite dramatic. My grandfather drove the school bus, so he was the one who took me in and told the teacher my name. The night before it had rained a lot and the country roads were muddy, causing our bus to arrive after everyone else was already there.

My grandpa walked me into the first-grade room and I nearly panicked. For the very first time in my life, I realized that there were forty or more kids the same size as me in the world. I hadn't been around large groups of kids much at all, and I don't think I had ever seen more than ten kids in my lifetime that were anywhere near the same size as me. I think I just sat there at the big old wooden desk all day long and looked around in total amazement.

My first, second, and third grade experiences were normal for these times. The fall before I started in the fourth grade, my family moved to a town named Montrose in Western Colorado, where my dad had taken

This is me at the age of 12, getting ready to drive one of my grandfather's old tractors.

a job with a farm machinery dealership. When I walked into my first day of school in this strange place, I faced another dramatic fact. Most of the kids were Hispanic. I had never encountered kids of any other race but my own in school before. I soon made new friends, however, and I had fun learning some of their customs. Since a majority of these Hispanic kids were Catholic, I would see my classmates at Mass, and this made it easier for me to fit in.

Each summer my two younger brothers and I would go to the family farm in Oklahoma and spend three months with our grandma and grandpa. We dearly loved to do this because our grandpa taught us to drive the tractors and old farm vehicles. The grandparents loved to have us and we learned to work hard and still have some fun doing simple things like flying a kite and fishing in creeks and the farm pond.

One of my grandfathers gave me his 1927 Model T Ford and the other one took it out to the farm and got it running. I learned to drive on the country roads at the ripe old age of ten. If you've never had to get all four coils singing and then set the spark lever just right so the engine wouldn't kick back and cause the hand crank to break your arm, you are not familiar with the art of starting a Model T. Learning how to start this temperamental old "T" and keep it running was the beginning of a great mechanical learning adventure for me and my brothers, one we have all made great use of throughout our lives.

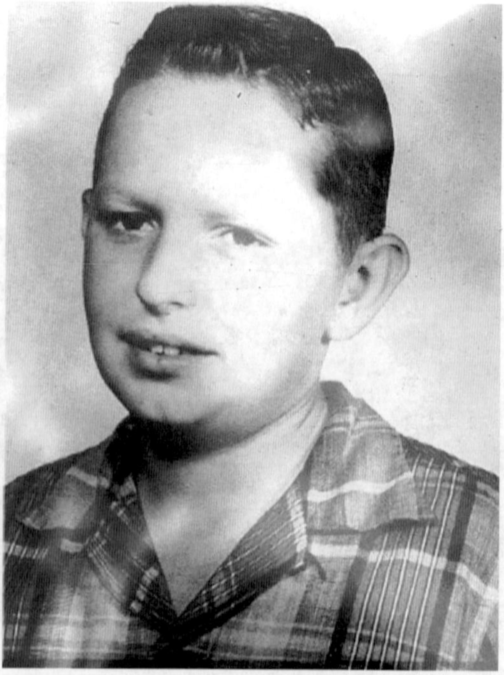

Until I turned thirteen, my life was no different than that of any other midwestern farmboy.

After spending my fourth- and fifth-grade school years living in Montrose with my parents and brothers, I moved in with my grandparents on the farm and returned to school in Custer City for my sixth-grade year. My decision had nothing to do with school and everything to do with the fact that I loved driving the old trucks and tractors we had on the farm. I liked that so well that I somehow talked my Mom and Dad into letting me stay on the farm. Grandpa and Grandma loved that, but I've hated myself for doing that since. It made my Mom cry. She said, "You're my child and I want to raise you. I don't want to leave you here." My Dad was all for it, though. He thought it would be neat for me to stay on the farm and help his parents, and so he and I won that battle.

Things didn't turn out as well as I expected that year. By the middle of the school year, I was missing my two brothers and my parents so badly I could hardly stand it. I saw my family at Christmastime, and I should've gone back to Montrose with them afterward, but I didn't. I stuck out the rest of the year on the farm and then rejoined my family in Montrose for my seventh-grade year.

After my parents had spent a total of four years living in Colorado, several of the owners of the farm machinery dealership where my dad worked died, and the other members decided to close the business. So my family moved back to Western Oklahoma. This time, however, we didn't go back to the farm but instead lived in Custer City. My mother and dad opened a farm machinery dealership of their own, similar to the one my dad had worked for in Colorado. This made it necessary for me to work in the repair shop after school and on Saturdays. At that time, I was in the eighth grade, and I didn't like to work all the time because my friends were always playing basketball.

I always felt being the oldest child and spending so much time helping my parents work robbed me of the experience of being a kid. I grew up much too fast and missed a lot of the slow development I needed. My dad was a very strict, serious, and no-nonsense kind of person, and I never felt I was allowed to act silly or just be a kid. As the oldest grandkid on both sides of the family, I felt as though I was expected to act mature, and I was especially careful to do this around my dad. I wanted to play basketball after school, but I had to get to the family business to get work done. I felt like I had little chance to have the fun of growing up that most other kids experienced. But my mother was more relaxed with me and my brothers, so it was easier for me to act my age around her without being so embarrassed.

When I was in the fifth and seventh grades in Colorado, my brother Ronnie and I were altar boys for the daily Mass before school. The church was only six to eight blocks from our house, and I enjoyed being an altar boy. The priests were very kind to us, and we were allowed to skip school when there was a funeral Mass. I enjoyed church and had a good relationship with the priests and nuns. During the summer, we went to Catechism and learned the teachings of the Catholic faith. I'm sure they taught us about heaven and hell and where we go when we die, but I don't really recall thinking about spirits or ghosts as a child.

CHAPTER TWO

Soul Travel Begins

One night when I was thirteen years old, something happened to me that was much stranger than anything I'd ever experienced before. After falling asleep in my bed, I awoke to find myself floating near the ceiling in the corner of the very small bedroom I shared with one of my brothers.

As I looked around the room, I could see all of these strange people floating by in prone positions, floating in and out of the room, right through the walls, floors, and ceiling. The more I stared in amazement at this sight, the more convinced I became that these were spirits. But they weren't the spirits of anyone I knew, and they didn't seem interested in me in the least. They clearly knew I was there, but they just slowly floated along past me.

When I tell you this, you need to know that I was *out of my body* at the time. As I mentioned before, I was floating near the ceiling above my bed. But when I looked down, I could see my body sleeping soundly in the bed below!

This began happening to me regularly during my nightly sleep. I had the most miserable nights anyone could imagine. Every time I would go to sleep or be near sleep, I would see spirits in the bedroom. Most of the time, there would be several of them as I floated in a corner near the ceiling. I could see myself and my younger brother lying in the bed below. Being terrified is putting it mildly; this was the scariest feeling I had ever had. I thought surely I had been a bad boy and the devil was coming to get me. I hated to go to bed knowing this same thing would happen again. I did not want the devil getting me, and of course I hated the terror that I felt each time I left my body.

For some time, all of these spirits pretty much ignored me. The first time that one of them came close and stared into my face, it scared me greatly. Usually the spirits I saw were always in motion, typically floating but occasionally walking. This was the first time I had seen any of these spirits remain more or less still, afloat in midair.

This particular spirit appeared to be a middle-aged female with long, light-colored hair. She just stared at my face for a long time, and I was very afraid she was going touch me, but she didn't. She just studied my face awhile and backed off and went on her way. She did not look like anyone I knew. I've thought about this spirit many times, and I don't think I've ever seen that particular face again. I think she just appeared to me that one time. She was definitely a woman; I could see her body, and she was dressed in the type of clothing I was accustomed to seeing women wear in those days.

Another reason that I hated these experiences was that it was always painful when my soul reentered my body. I didn't want to go through that ordeal again, either. Many times when I woke up the next morning, my body would feel like someone had beaten me up badly. I could not understand this. I didn't understand what was happening, but I knew that my soul was up around the ceiling and my body was lying in bed because I could see it there beside my brother. But I could not understand why it caused such a great bang that hurt so badly when my soul rushed back into my body. It made my body just ache all over. I was so sore that every limb hurt, and that made it hard to get out of bed and move around. I hardly had the strength to put my pants on in the morning.

My dad would tell me that I needed to go to bed earlier and get more sleep so I could go to school and do my work. But the problem wasn't that I was tired. My body felt like someone had just taken a baseball bat and beaten me all over with it, or like I had just worked at something terribly hard, abusing my body in the process. I could not understand how that could've happened, because I knew my body hadn't done anything except lie there in bed; I assumed it was asleep the whole time because it was always lying still. Even today, I still don't understand how this could've happened.

My mother was the only person I would tell about my terrible, scary ordeals. She would say, "I guess you had a bad dream." When something hurts, we tend to not do the same thing again. So I started trying to somehow make the landings easier when my soul returned to my body. It took several years before I was finally able to slow the travel speed as I approached my body and achieve a soft landing. It was very difficult, but I concentrated on stopping before I hit my body so I wouldn't hit it so hard. Finally, I was able to control my soul enough to make softer landings that didn't hurt as much.

At this time, I had never heard of out-of-body experiences nor had I known of anything like this happening to anyone else. The first couple of times I looked down and saw myself lying in bed beside my younger brother, it was hard to believe that the body in the bed was me, although I knew it had to be. I recognized my brother, but the guy lying on the other side of the bed looked like a stranger, and that feeling was quite disappointing. He looked nothing like me. It was hard to accept that I looked nothing like the image I saw in a mirror. Looking in the mirror, I thought I was handsome, or at least pleasant-looking. But this fellow I saw below me in my bed was ugly and had a big nose; he really seemed like someone I had never seen before. It took awhile to finally accept that it was me. I was greatly disappointed, to put it mildly.

While in a floating state, I would not be able to move any part of my body. I couldn't talk or do anything that would entice my soul to come down from the ceiling and get back into my body. It seemed to *want* to stay floating around the room, scared almost to death. But I don't ever recall leaving my body more than once a night.

I didn't feel anything approaching a physical sensation when I was floating. The old house in Oklahoma was cold at night; it had no heat and there was a constant cold wind blowing outside. The windows weren't insulated. In fact, the gap around the window sill would let snow blow in, and many mornings we would have inches of snow on top of the blankets at the bottom of the bed. My brother and I would have many layers of blankets over ourselves to keep us warm so we could sleep. But when I was floating above my bed, I wasn't dressed in anything but bedclothes and I never felt cold. I was comfortable, never hot or cold. I felt no physical sensations at all, really.

As for other types of feelings, I experienced nothing but fear while I was out of body. I was just afraid that these spirits and the devil were coming to take me to hell. When I saw these other spirits, I wasn't seeing them with my eyes. I could see myself asleep below and my eyes were closed. But I could see them as clearly as I saw anyone. Perhaps they were in a different dimension, but I surely saw them quite clearly.

After months and months of trying everything to stop my out-of-body experiences, I learned to make a gruff sound deep in my throat. This would sometimes awaken my brother and bring a poke in the ribs, a slap, or some gesture that would immediately cause my soul to return to my body. That was what I wanted. I wanted to be safely back in my body as soon as possible. My brother said the noise I made didn't sound human. He said it was a deep growl like an animal would make. My little trick didn't stop me from leaving my body at night, of course, but at least it gave me an easy way to end these terrifying nightly experiences once they'd started.

CHAPTER THREE

Hot Rods, Motorcycles, and Semi-Trucks

One of my teenage loves was building drag race cars. My brother and I were lucky to have our dad's tractor shop to work in. We were both good mechanics by this time, as well as fair welders. We would do things like installing a big, souped-up V-8 engine with several carburetors in an old Ford coupe. After adding a few extras like a roll bar, we were ready to go to the races. This was so much fun that several of our friends joined in and we always had several cars under construction.

My dad wasn't crazy about us racing, but he said he would rather see us on a track with some adult supervision than have us running down the public highways at over a hundred miles per hour. We were using a lot of his gas, oil, and electricity, as well as his welding rod, but at least he always knew where we were.

When my brother and I weren't working on one car or another, we kept ourselves busy with an old motorcycle. I had a well-worn 1947 Harley Davidson and he had an old Indian. These two cycles required that we spend more time repairing them than riding.

My Harley was a fun toy to ride, but if you rode any type of motorcycle in the late 1950s, you were looked down on as a sort of lowlife or undesirable. There were several girls I was interested in dating during this period. If their fathers knew me, they would say, "Don't you dare get on his motorcycle." They were more afraid of their daughters being seen on a motorcycle with a lowlife than they were of the possibility of me actually crashing.

One Sunday afternoon, I rode my old Harley out in the country to the house of a girl that I liked and had already been out with on several dates. We went for a short ride down a dirt country road, and when I tried to turn around in the loose sand, I killed the engine. I couldn't get it started up right away, and the girl told me she needed to be home soon. Finally, after the engine had cooled somewhat, we were able to get started and be on our way again. All of a sudden, this girl screamed and pointed to her white tennis shoe, which was covered with black engine oil that had leaked out. She said, "My dad is going to kill me! He just bought me these new shoes." When we got back to her house, she stepped off of the bike. I hit the road in a hurry before my date's parents had a chance to come out and see her oily shoe.

One night in an adjoining town with a movie theater, I saw one of the best-looking girls in town. She was the most popular girl in the whole county. She and some of her friends were standing on the sidewalk. I had never thought of asking her for a date because she was very popular. She ran around with all of the football stars and studs from her school and the surrounding schools, and that kept her plenty busy with dates. But that night, I asked her if she would like to ride on my old Harley. Some of the other girls started telling her to go ahead. I think some of them even made dares for her to do it.

In those days, the girls wore tight skirts down below their knees; this was considered dressy attire at the time. This girl had on a very tight skirt because she was dressed up for a weekend night out; everyone came to town to go to the movies on the weekend. I remember her putting one foot up on the foot peg and trying to get her other leg across the seat to climb onto the cycle. That just couldn't happen with a tight skirt on. So after a couple of tries, she reached down, took hold of the bottom of her skirt, and pulled it up over her butt. Her bare legs were simply shining as she threw one of them over the seat. After she had crawled completely onto the cycle, we took off down the street. I knew by this time that several guys and girls had congregated on the sidewalk. As I rode off with the best-looking girl in the county, her skirt pulled up and her legs shining in the moonlight, I knew that I was the envy of most of the other guys standing on the sidewalk. That was kind of fun!

My high school experience with motor vehicles wasn't all fun and games, though. I actually started driving a semi-truck and trailer for my dad's business when I was only fifteen years old. He needed help in delivering equipment to his customers. Back then, all the local cops knew everybody around. They knew I didn't have a driver's license, but they also knew I was out there helping my dad and that he truly needed the help, so they never said anything. I was very careful when I drove the truck and trailer, and I completed many deliveries for my dad along the Route 66 long before I could legally drive. My dad wouldn't let me drive into Oklahoma City until I got my driver's license, though.

CHAPTER FOUR

Soul Travel Continues

My out-of-body experiences continued through my high school years, as if I didn't have enough to keep myself occupied with during the waking hours. Since that first terrifying night when I was thirteen, I'd continued to have very similar experiences almost nightly. However, once I'd grown a bit used to the strangeness of the mere fact that I was floating outside of my own body, nothing earthshattering or even particularly memorable happened during any of these hundreds of soul travels. Essentially, the same experiences that I've already described were repeated over and over again. I would find myself floating up near the ceiling of my room in a prone position, watching spirits float in and out of view. Nothing really new or different happened, and I never saw a single spirit that I recognized.

After this had been happening regularly for two years, I finally decided that maybe the spirits I was seeing weren't so bad. For one thing, none of them had ever tried to hurt me. Most seemed to be moving as if they were traveling somewhere, and they appeared to be busy, never stopping to visit or just hang around. I don't remember generally noticing differences in their genders; they just seemed to be people all going their own way.

Sometimes, though, one of these spirits would come right up and sort of look me over—that was always scary. At first, I would be so terrified that I would rush back into my body to feel safe. As time went on, I started to become unable to return to my body when I wanted to. And when I did finally return, I would hit my body so hard that it would jump off the bed or at least bounce up in the air. Sometimes I would wake as my body was in mid-jump or mid-bounce. It would even wake my brother up!

Around the time I was eighteen and close to finishing high school, I finally learned that I would not leave my body at night unless I fell asleep on my back. I don't know any reason, physical or otherwise, why sleeping on my stomach or my side would prevent soul travel from happening. Evidently, it was just something in my mindset that I'd picked up somewhere: If I'm not on my back, soul travel can't happen.

I had slept on my back for years, but no more. After learning to sleep on my side or stomach, it seemed I had eliminated the experiences—I could actually sleep through the night without leaving my body. This approach worked really well for quite a while. Then one night, while sleeping on my stomach in a travel trailer during a camping trip, I left my body—and the area—for some time. I was scared my nightly out-of-body experiences would start to happen again, but they didn't. This was just about the only soul travel experience I had for a period of quite a few years.

Now, over fifty years later, I absolutely cannot go to sleep on my back no matter how hard I try. And I actually really want to now, because after all these years, I see these out-of-body experiences as wonderful. I would love to have a soul travel experience every night now and keep learning, but that is not happening in my older age. I've tried many times—concentrating, meditating, doing anything I can think of—and nothing has worked.

CHAPTER FIVE

My First and Last Semester in College

I graduated from high school in the spring of 1959 and in the fall, I enrolled in Southwestern State College in Weatherford, about twenty miles from Custer City. (These days, the college is known as Southwestern Oklahoma State University.) I was really surprised by what college life was like and quickly became very unhappy with it. I'd never liked high school anyway, and all I ever wanted from school was to get out of it. I always thought, "Let me out of here and I'll show the world how to make a million dollars."

College certainly opened my eyes. I had one male teacher that was gay, and I had never seen a gay person in my life—at least as far as I knew. I could hardly accept it at that time. This teacher liked four or five of the pretty boys, so to speak, and they would always sit right up in the front row in the classroom. He spent most of his time visiting with them. I wanted to be as far away from him as I could be, but I had no choice—I had to take this class. I sat in the back of the room and learned almost nothing. I hated for his class to come every day because of his relationship with the pretty boys. This only increased my already negative feelings about school.

Then I had another male teacher who was pretty young and just so gung ho about his classes that it seemed like something might be wrong with him. He had a policy that if you were absent from his class three times during the semester, you would automatically fail. One day we had a terrible flood on campus, and people were walking around with water up past their ankles. I really wanted to just go home, but it was time for this gung ho teacher's class. I thought to myself that as crazy as this guy was and as stupidly as he acted—his behavior was stupid in my mind, anyway—he was liable to be there and count anyone who didn't show up as absent. Sure enough, he held the whole hour-long class that day. I was one of only three students who showed up, and everyone else was counted absent that day.

That kind of turned me against school too. I thought that college professors were supposed to be intelligent, reasonable people. They were supposed to be telling us how to live and what we're going to need to know to get along in life. But this gung ho teacher seemed to be teaching me that regardless of how deep the flood waters got, he would use them as a chance to rack up absences in his book and flunk students. I thought that if this was the kind of person I needed to show me how to get along in the world, then I didn't want any part of it.

I took my final tests at the end of the semester, but to this day, I don't know whether I passed any of them or not. I never even went back the next week to find out what my grades were. I just dropped out of school and went to work with my father and mother in their farm machinery business in Custer City. I'd had all the college life that I could stand. My parents had moved into another house in town by this point, but they still owned the small house where I'd lived with them when I was in high school. I bought that house from them and settled back into it.

CHAPTER SIX

Starting a Family at Nineteen

Custer City was a small town, only a couple of blocks long. It had a grocery, a drug store, and a car dealership down the street from my family's farm machinery business. One thing that always caught my eye around town was a hot-looking '56 Chevy that belonged to an old local bootlegger named Jack. Along with all of the guys in town who were into drag racing, I'd had my eyes on that car for a long time.

The car caught my attention more than ever one day in 1960 around Thanksgiving when I saw it parked on the street by my parents' business and the Chevy dealership. I knew everyone in town, so it was a surprise to see a girl I didn't know was sitting in it. I went over to ask her why she was in Jack's car and she informed me she was his granddaughter, Delores. She told me that she and her sister were moving in with their grandparents and that they would soon be enrolling in the local high school.

Both girls had been living with their mother and their stepfather, who worked in the oil fields. At that time, they'd been moving around about every six months—and sometimes even more often—following oil field construction. Delores was going to be a senior in high school that year, and she wanted to be in the same class with the same classmates for her whole senior year. That was the main reason she and her sister wanted to move in with her Grandpa Jack and her grandma. I asked her if she wanted to drag race with me, and she said no, she wouldn't do that with her granddad's car and didn't know how to race anyway.

This is me at the age of 21, fine-tuning a modified 1932 Ford Coupe.

Not long after that we started dating and our relationship became serious pretty quickly. We were married on July 1, 1961. I was 19 years of age, and Delores was 17. We lived together in the house I'd bought from my parents, and I continued to work for my parents' farm machinery business. We had a son in 1963 and named him Chris.

My parents' business fell on hard times and failed in 1964. I was now out of a job, and for the first time in my life, I went looking for one. The first job I tried to get was selling new cars at a dealership in Clinton, Oklahoma. The owners of this dealership said they would be willing to give me a try. This was a great job because I would get to dress in nice clothes and work all day long without even getting my hands dirty. I would get just as excited as the customers when we made a deal and they got to drive a brand-new car home. In the meantime, Delores took a job as a bookkeeper with a local bakery. We still lived in Custer City, so I made a fifteen-mile commute to work each day.

My longtime connections in Custer City and Thomas served me well in this new job. I went back to both towns and talked up the business with a lot of folks I had gotten to know while growing up. In doing this, I managed to bring a lot of these folks in as customers for the car dealership. My bosses loved this, of course, because I was actually going out beyond their normal trade area and bringing in new business. So not only was I very happy with my new job, but my employers were very happy with me. After I'd worked for this dealership for about a year, one of my bosses at the dealership sold me his house in Clinton and we moved in.

Not too long after this, in 1966, my daughter Raquel was born. As I mentioned before, my out-of-body experiences had stopped almost completely once I had trained myself to sleep on my side or my stomach instead of my back at about the age of eighteen. It wasn't until around the time of my daughter's birth that they began to return. They began happening to me almost every night that I slept on my back.

I hadn't really discussed my out-of-body experiences with Delores until after we were married. She seemed to believe me when I talked to her about this and she was never critical, but she didn't really seem interested in talking about it much. I guess I didn't press the matter because I still didn't know how to explain it. I didn't have the language to describe the experience. I had never heard of out-of-body experiences or soul travel at the time. I didn't really discuss these experiences with anyone else, either, because I didn't understand what they were myself.

After a second year of working at the car dealership, I had the opportunity to become the co-owner of a Pontiac-Buick dealership in Weatherford, where I'd gone to college. This town was only twenty miles from where I had grown up, which meant I could count on even more of my old friends coming in and doing business with me.

Looking back, I now know that I was too young and inexperienced to run a business of my own at this point in my life, but back then, I was just too gung ho to worry much about the difficulties that lie ahead. I'd been heavily involved in the Jaycees for several years, and I'd taken a Dale Carnegie class that had taught me that there was nothing I couldn't do if I believed in myself, worked hard, and kept my thoughts and attitudes positive.

I had to grow up in a hurry and learn to deal with General Motors, finance companies, and bankers. It's tough when you realize that you have several employees and their families who rely on you to deliver their paychecks and provide them with a good livelihood. You had to make several thousand dollars of profit every day to keep the place going. In those circumstances, you learn to be business savvy very quickly, even if you're very young. I enjoyed the business and dearly loved helping raise my two little kids.

I commuted from Clinton to Weatherford for over a year. Then one day, an exterminator who lived in Weatherford but who did a lot of work around Clinton contacted me to see if I was interested in trading houses with him. The switch would make both of our lives easier, and our houses were of comparable value, so I agreed to his proposal and relocated my family to Weatherford.

It wasn't too far of a drive to the family farm, and I soon began to think about leasing the farm's operation from my eighty-five-year-old grandfather. He wanted to slow down a bit because my grandmother had died and he now had to live alone and cook for himself for the first time in his life. He didn't want to leave the farm he'd been born on, the same farm where my father and I had also been born. I wanted to help my grandfather, but I also dearly loved to till the soil, plant the seeds, and see the crops grow. And I loved raising animals too; I loved to watch them as they grew up and had their own babies.

I talked to my dad and uncles about my idea of leasing the farm, and they thought it would be good for me. Maybe I could even make a little profit and have my father and my granddad work for me. It would be good for my grandfather to be out working everyday, and he wouldn't have strangers on his farm, as would have happened if he leased the farm to someone else. His life didn't change much since he still took care of the cattle, drove the tractors, and did field work every day. I would show him a particular way I wanted to till or plant a field and he would agree. Then as soon as I would drive away, he did the job in the same way he had for the previous seventy years. I soon figured out that he knew more about farming than I did anyway, so we had a lot of fun together.

Meanwhile, there was a pretty fast pace to working in the car dealership all day—sell this, sell that, get this car fixed, and deal with the guy who's complaining because his car was supposed to be ready at ten o'clock and it's eleven now and his wife is waiting and the car's not done. It was just bang-bang-bang high pressure all day long. When evening came and I drove the twenty miles out to the farm, it was like a mini-vacation.

I spent a lot of Sundays out on the farm, driving the tractor, checking on the cattle, and so on. It was a real getaway to go work on the farm. It was food for the mind, so to speak, to get out there and get away from the telephone and people hollering and complaining about something all the time. I was even getting away from myself and the way I would complain to the salesmen that they weren't selling enough.

One of my greatest delights began when my two kids grew old enough to go to the farm with me. They would ask a million questions about everything. They would ask why a cow was black but her baby was red. I'd try to explain the daddy was red. They would say, "Well, if the mama is black and the daddy is red, why isn't it half-red and half-black?"

These times were truly great—three or four generations could get together and till the soil, plant seeds, and care for the livestock. It was great for my son to get to know my grandfather. Bonds were made on that farm that would last forever. Years later, when my son was thirty and had been living in a big city for a number of years, he said to me, "Dad, I sure hope to have a small place at the edge of town where I can raise some cattle again, because I have such fond memories of growing up caring for them."

Another thing that was dear to my heart during these times was a female boxer dog named Honey. All of us have probably had a favorite pet or two in our lives that seem to be members of the family. Honey was certainly that to us. We had gotten her as a baby pup, and the kids and I played with her every day for several years. We all loved Honey, and the feeling was mutual.

I remember one time we had gone to Colorado in the winter to ski. We had left one of the neighbors to feed and take care of Honey. She had a warm place in a building outside the house to sleep in. She was fine with that. However, when we got back four days later, she was very sick with a case of distemper and I had to take her to the vet. I asked the neighbor why he hadn't taken her to the vet, and he said that he knew we would be back soon. The vet told me that Honey was very, very sick and one reason for this was that she had no energy left because she had not eaten. In his opinion, she would not survive this trauma.

The vet said the only thing I could possibly do would be to try to force some food down Honey's throat. But I would have to physically force it down, because she was too weak to chew or swallow any food. So I took her home and made her a bed inside the house, near the stove where it was warm. I forced hamburger meat down her throat with my finger at least twice a day. Sometimes I could only get a little bit down there, but I kept at it. Honey ended up getting her strength back and getting well again. I've always thought this probably helped us to share a special bond.

CHAPTER SEVEN

The White Light

The next major shock wave—one of the most significant experiences of my life—shot through my entire being. I was somewhere around twenty-eight years old when this happened. After awakening from sleep in the middle of the night, I lay on my back trying to go back to sleep when I felt my soul leaving my body and traveling through darkness.

I realized I was in a long, dark tunnel and that I was continuing to move further into it. This was the first time I'd ever left my home during an out-of-body experience. I was moving slowly through this tunnel and experiencing some very frightening feelings. I've always had a little bit of claustrophobia—not so bad that I have ever lost control of myself, but the fear was always there in the background at least a little bit. I was starting to get some feelings of claustrophobia as I moved through this long, dark tunnel. I thought to myself, "What kind of a deal is this? Am I falling into a bottomless hole that I'll never get out of?" But I actually wasn't going down. I had the sensation of going sideways through this tunnel. I kept moving through this tunnel for a good amount of time.

About the time I was getting really scared, I saw a light. After studying this light and my surroundings for a time, I realized I was in a round tunnel and the light was at the other end. The closer I moved toward this light, the brighter it became and the more of a pull I could feel. It was like a huge magnet exerting a force on my whole being. The closer I came, the stronger the feeling of being pulled grew.

This was the warmest, most loving feeling I have ever experienced, even to this very day. It was like a strong magnet was pulling me toward it, and the closer I got to it, the stronger and warmer the pull grew. I was feeling better and better, and the light kept getting bigger and brighter. Now I was finding the experience to be wonderful. I didn't know what the light was, but the feeling it gave me was warm and peaceful and fantastic. It pulled me right to the end of the tunnel until I was right on the edge of it. The light was a very bright white with a tinge of gold coming out its middle. That was my impression anyway.

The light was so bright that I couldn't look at the center of it. I had to look around its edges. It was such a warm feeling. I felt like I wanted to go there; I wanted to be there. It was as if I had finally come home. I felt that this light was my home, that this was where I belonged. It felt as if I had been on a long trip somewhere, doing something else, and now I'd finally come back home and was glad to be there.

As I approached the light, I realized there were three beings standing just outside the end of this tunnel. The first one was the closest to me, the second was standing behind the first, and the third was standing partially behind the second one. All three made me feel very welcome, as though they were some kind of welcoming committee. I became aware that I was enjoying total peace and a loving feeling unlike anything I had ever known before. These three beings were dressed in light-colored robes. Although I felt they were male, the only thing I had to base that on was their body build and short hair. I did not recognize them as anyone I had previously known.

The third being seemed kind of clownish compared to the first two, who were more serious. The appearance of the third one suggested that he was thinking, "Come over and we will have some fun." As I kept slowly drawing closer to the end of the tunnel, it looked as if the vastness of this area beyond the tunnel went on forever. The beings were beckoning me to come closer, so I moved up to the very end of the tunnel. The three kept trying to get me to step out, but somehow I knew deep down inside that if I took that one last step, I could not return. By now I wanted to stay here, however, because the white light was so warm and loving and so much at total peace.

The light was so bright that I felt I could not look into the center of it. I realized that this white brilliance with a golden glow mixed into it was God, and I knew that he was so glorious that I couldn't look directly at him. This entire place had a tremendous power that kept pulling me toward it. It was easy to tell there was no want for anything here because the total love and peacefulness of the light engulfed everything. I just wanted to stand there and be cradled by its soothing effect.

Somehow I knew that if I traveled into the light, I would be shown far greater things than I had ever known. I felt there were massive structures and many beings beyond the vast area I could see outside the tunnel. The three beings were like a welcoming committee, as I mentioned before, and they were doing their job well. I did feel most welcome. They tried to get me to stay, and I wanted to. The loving pull toward the light continued as I stood at the very end of the tunnel. The space from which the light seemed to originate appeared to be more vast than anything I had ever seen before. It was bigger than the entire great outdoors, and it gave me the sensation that it might go on forever.

I kept saying I couldn't stay, that I had to go back because I had two children who needed me very much. I must go back and take care of them and raise them, I explained. The beings, the loving and pure white light, the totally peaceful feeling, and the lack of want or need for anything made me want to take the last step out of the tunnel and stay here forever. But I knew I could not go back if I took that one last step. I kept saying, "No, I cannot stay. I cannot go in any deeper toward the light. I must go back. I must raise my children." I said this over and over, "I must go back."

After a time, I realized I was going to return for sure. Now I wasn't so torn or scared, but I still didn't want to go back to the turmoil and problems of life in the physical plane. I liked this place; it was peaceful like I thought Earth should be. I felt that this was where I belonged. This was truly home and I wanted to stay forever. The white light felt like total knowledge and total truth. Although this feeling was all-loving, I knew my most important mission was to raise my two children. I returned through the tunnel at a much faster pace than I had traveled through it the first time. It was a good feeling to have been asked to stay and to know that I was wanted in this awesome place.

The experience of seeing this light and feeling this tremendous love made me a better person. It truly made me want to perform only good acts and do no harm to anyone. I didn't want to take a chance of not being asked to stay at a later date. It also made me realize life goes on after this short stay on this physical plane, because the three beings were as much alive as I was. They were living and doing their jobs, much as I was doing mine on the earthly plane. After returning to my body, I didn't sleep any more that night.

At the time of this experience, I still did not know what it meant to be out of body, but I was starting to get some idea. I was anxious to learn more about my visit to this glorious place and share my new realization that the soul and body are not one but two separate things. I had never been a reader, but my recent experiences changed that. I had to learn more about how the soul could travel and visit what I think was heaven while the body stayed in bed and never moved.

I read a book by Robert Monroe called *Journeys Out of the Body* that finally explained some of what was happening to me. Then I read *The Search for Bridey Murphy*, the story of an American housewife named Virginia Tighe who remembered past-life experiences under hypnosis. This book was quite popular forty years ago or so. Virginia actually traveled to the house in England where she had lived as Bridey Murphy, one of her past incarnations. The foundation was all that was left, but she could walk around and describe what each of the rooms had looked like. She remembered the names of all her family members from this life too, and she could describe what each of them had been like. Books like these were opening a whole new world for me. I realized I wasn't the only one having these unusual experiences.

"Out-of-body experiences," "soul travel," "reincarnation"—these words and phrases were all new to me. But I had experienced hundreds of soul separations, or at least that's what I thought they were, because I had spent a lot of time near the bedroom ceiling looking down at my body while I watched spirits moving past me. The idea of reincarnation started to make sense to me: The soul lived forever and used different bodies for assorted learning experiences through the ages. This concept of having multiple life situations over a long span of time became real to me.

I had been taught all my life that we must be nearly perfect, we must be free from sin, and we must love our neighbors as we love ourselves in order to get to heaven. Not only that, but we must do all of this in a very short lifetime of between thirty and seventy years. Before my experience in the tunnel, I would listen to different priests and preachers rant and rave that unless we all learn to get every action and every thought perfect in this short lifetime, we will be damned to hell for eternity. I remember thinking I had better learn a whole lot more in the second half of my lifetime than I had learned in the first half, because I knew that deep down I was prejudiced against everyone who didn't think exactly as I did.

I knew for sure that my thoughts weren't all perfect nor were my actions toward my fellow man. Overall, the actions I'd taken in my life up to this point were probably close to the bottom of the scale, but they were perhaps more typical than I realized at that point. I was not a bad person. I just thought that my community of predominantly Anglo-Saxon churchgoers in the middle of the Bible Belt surely had everything figured out just right.

I knew it was a fact that some of the women in church spent more time looking at the other women than they did paying attention to the service, trying to figure out if they had ever seen that blue dress before, or wondering if that hat was brand-new or thinking that maybe it looked like one they saw at a garage sale last week. And heaven forbid if a visitor might have sat in the particular pew where you have parked yourself for the past twenty years. This kind of tragedy blew your mind and no one would expect you to be able to concentrate on the Mass if you were faced with such a dilemma.

If anyone else in the world had a different way than this to serve the Lord, surely they were on the wrong track. After all, if we had a little trouble understanding the Latin portion of the Mass, it was easy to take a short nap. I started to realize the many hours I had spent on bended knees repeating the *Our Father* and *Hail Mary* prayers over and over had really done very little good, for me at least. I remember what a hollow feeling I had when it hit me that the hundreds of rosaries I had said all those years were not going to get me into heaven. It took some time for me to accept the fact I was going to have to do something different to make the grade, so to speak.

This was the first time the golden rule—"Do unto others as you would have them do unto you"—started to make an impression on me. The scariest part of this was to consider how much extra effort it might take to put this kind of lifestyle in motion. I had been comfortable through the years doing things that would help me and the family, but I wasn't sure I had time to worry about anyone else.

I started thinking that I should spend my prayer time thinking good thoughts for all of humankind and asking the higher powers to show me ways I could help my fellow man. I soon discovered this thinking would give me a warm feeling, and I looked forward to being able to pray in this new manner as often as I could. It was very pleasant. Instead of worrying one of the children might get hurt or run over by a car and then being scared into saying the *Hail Mary* fifty times to prevent something bad from happening, I found it much nicer to think that the kids would return from school every day with enthusiastic stories of what new things they had learned. I would think good thoughts about how they would grow and mature into good, productive citizens and how their spiritual guides were always there to help them do this.

I soon started to lose the prejudices I had learned as a child and carried with me ever since—biases against anyone of a different color than me and anyone with customs or religious beliefs different than my own. For the first time, I thought I had really found the true path to heaven. After seeing the glorious place where love abounds and want, need, discomfort, and jealousy don't exist, I certainly wanted to mend my ways and earn the right to be there the next time.

CHAPTER EIGHT

Floating Farther From Home

Soon after my trip through the tunnel toward the white light, I started having out-of-body experiences more frequently, and they became more interesting. Although it would still scare me when I realized my soul had separated and was floating above my body, I learned not to fight this situation and sort of just go with the flow of the experience. Other than my journey through the tunnel, I don't remember my soul floating any farther away than the ceiling of the bedroom before this time. This now changed as I began to float through the walls of the house and travel from room to room. It was a very delightful feeling to be able to move through a solid object with no difficulty whatsoever. I seemed to always float in a prone position, as though I was lying in bed.

During one of these flotation excursions, I realized I was heading straight toward the water heater located near the kitchen. I thought to myself, "There's no way I can go through steel, glass, and boiling water." But a few seconds later, I floated through the middle of this water heater just as easily as I floated through the walls. Moving through solid objects like this was nearly the oddest experience I had ever had. I knew that these objects were impossible for a body to pass through. I knew my physical body was lying on the bed, but I also knew that I could pass through these solid objects as if they were no different than thin air. After returning to my body and awakening, I remembered hearing about Jesus just appearing in places as though he had come through the walls or ceiling.

I remember thinking that this ability to move through solid objects was really neat and that maybe I could even learn to travel outside the house. After many tries and many failures, I finally was able to get through the roof above my bedroom. This was really different, because instead of just looking at the inside of my home, I could now see the grove of locust trees in the backyard and the stars and clouds in the nighttime sky.

It seems that with each new barrier that I overcame in my soul travels, a new set of problems came into being—almost the same situation that always seems to happen in the physical state. The first new problem was now that I could leave the house and get out into the big world, I was scared to go any farther than two or three feet above the roof. Everything in the neighborhood looked the same as what I saw every day—the neighboring houses, the streets, the parked vehicles, and even the animals running around at times. They were the same kinds of things I would see in the daytime, and once in a while, I would even see a beautiful moon in the night sky.

Although by this point I had read about people soul-traveling to different cities, I was scared that maybe I wouldn't be able to find my way back to where my body was. It took about a year to overcome this fear of getting lost, but finally I felt I was ready to try some long-distance movement.

Now I was faced with a brand-new problem. To this point in my many years of traveling outside of my body, I had almost always slowly floated around the house or stayed very close to the roof; the only exception to this was my experience in the tunnel with the white light at the end, in which I had been pulled by a force that felt almost magnetic. Now that I had overcome the fear of not being able to find my way back to my body, I realized that I didn't know how to propel myself. I tried walking, but that didn't work. I was stuck just above the roof. I started reading again and learned that others had experienced this same problem. They had learned to propel themselves by using a swimming motion. And some could simply think about a faraway place they wanted to visit and they'd instantly be there.

Going far away from home was much too scary an idea for me, as it had taken a lot of time just to get used to the idea that I couldn't see my body lying in bed. It was a lot of hard work, but the swimming motion did work a little. After several months of practicing this every time my soul left my body, the farthest I could get was a block or two from my house.

Over a period of time, I learned to feel comfortable hovering close to the roof. Although I could not see my body, I knew where it was—in my bedroom at the end of the house—and I felt I could get back to it quickly if I needed to. I thought about how neat it would be to travel to a beautiful place like London or Paris. But I was careful not to desire such a trip too much, because I wasn't even sure which direction those cities were from me. My fear of not being able to find my way back was very strong.

CHAPTER NINE

The Turmoil of Divorce and Remarriage

I was thirty-five years old before I learned about soul mates. Life was going along pretty normally when one day Ronald Nabors, a friend of mine, drove on to my car lot, which started a chain reaction of events that changed my life more than anything else that has ever happened to me. As Ronald was getting out of his pickup truck, I noticed there was a very attractive lady with him. He introduced her as Jeannie, his oldest sister. This took me by surprise, because I had met Ronald's younger sister, younger brother, and his mother, and none of them had ever mentioned an older sister. I remember telling him, "I don't believe this gal is really your sister." He replied, "Sure, she is." He then told me that she had been married for ten years, had a four-year-old daughter, and lived almost 500 miles away in St. Louis, Missouri.

I visited with both of them for ten or fifteen minutes, and I must say, I was very intrigued by Jeannie. She was very pretty, but it felt as though there was something else that caused me to want to visit with her. They left and I did not see her again, although he would come by my car lot every week or so, intrigued by the vehicles that I had to sell.

As the months went on, I found myself thinking about Jeannie and wondering about this mysterious feeling that kept haunting me. I would ask Ronald about his sister from time to time and he would say he had not seen her, but that he knew she was all right because she had talked to other family members.

The next year, 1976, I sold my automobile business and started a new business selling used heavy trucks in Oklahoma City, which was quite a commute from my home—sixty-five miles each way. After ten years of selling cars and doing the same thing every day, I was getting tired of worrying about all of my customers' rattles and squeaks and maybe a small bit of wind noise someone might have heard out of one window of their car. I was very proud and honored to have the customers, and I wanted to take good care of them, but after a period of time, I just got tired of worrying about every tiny little problem that cropped up.

I had sold several heavy trucks in the past two or three years. I enjoyed doing this and learned I didn't have to worry about a small scratch in the paint or weird noises the vehicle might be making. If the truck would do the job that the customer needed and was at a price he could handle, it was an easy sale. It was also enjoyable to sell something that would help the customer earn money in his own business.

I hired my friend Ronald to work with me in my new business. That July, he told me Jeannie was coming for a two-week visit and that she was planning to have lunch with him. Sure enough, the next week she showed up to take her brother to lunch, and they invited me to go along. As lunch progressed, we visited about our families and about high school days. Jeannie and I discovered that even though we hadn't met until the previous year, we had actually grown up only fifty miles apart. One big reason that our paths never crossed was that our schools did not participate in the same basketball conferences. Another was that the closest movie theater for each of us was in different towns. In the late fifties and early sixties, farm kids didn't venture much farther from home than the closest movie house.

After lunch, when Jeannie was preparing to leave, we both voiced our feelings that we hoped to see each other again soon and visit some more. A couple of days went by, and then the phone rang at work. I answered and was delighted to hear her voice. Her brother was not there at the time, so the two of us ended up having a long conversation. After hanging up the phone, I had this strong, mysterious feeling that she was my oldest and dearest friend. I also felt sad that I couldn't go on talking to her forever.

In the next two weeks, we saw each other a couple more times, and it seemed as if she enjoyed our time together as much as I did. Although I did not know it at the time, I later discovered that Jeannie had almost the same crazy, mysterious feeling that I had experienced ever since our first lunch together. She later described this feeling as having suddenly found her soul mate, although she hadn't consciously been looking for one.

Soon Jeannie's vacation was over and she returned to her home in St. Louis. In the days that followed, I experienced a sad, empty feeling as though an integral part of my being had disappeared. This troubled me greatly since I was married and had two children whom I loved dearly. My Catholic faith made this situation harder because I had been taught for years that it is an enormous sin to have feelings for a woman that was not your wife.

As each day passed, my inner turmoil became worse. I would spend my nights thinking instead of sleeping. On one hand, I missed my new friend so much I was miserable. At the same time, I was torn by the idea that something might happen that would hurt my two kids. As with most loving fathers, I would have gladly given my life for those kids; caring for them was my main purpose in life.

After several long-distance telephone conversations with my new friend, I learned she was experiencing the same feelings I was. Jeannie could not explain her feelings any more than I could, especially in light of the fact that we had only met each other a short time ago and had only visited a few times. By now, we both realized our feelings could not be ignored, and this mystery seemed to grow deeper with each passing day. After two weeks, Jeannie's husband took a weekend trip without her. Jeannie took this opportunity to gather her daughter, her dog, and a few clothes, and then flew to Oklahoma City to start a new life. That same weekend, I sent her brother Ronald—who, as I've mentioned, was now my employee—to St. Louis with a moving truck that I owned as part of my business. He packed the truck with the belongings Jeannie had indicated that she wanted to keep, and he delivered this load to an apartment in Oklahoma City that I had rented out for Jeannie.

Jeannie enrolled her daughter in preschool as Julie Schmitz; even though this wasn't Julie's legal last name yet, no one in the school system ever questioned it or asked to see a birth certificate. Jeannie acquired a job as secretary for an insurance company. Although it was wonderful to be able to see her and visit with her during the day, my life fell into complete turmoil. I was living with a wife whom I loved, two kids I adored, and a boxer dog that I was crazy about, but it was clear to me that Jeannie and I truly belonged with one another. After two months of sleepless nights and daily agitation over my unexplained feelings, I did the hardest thing I have ever had to do in my life. I filed for divorce from Delores and walked out of my house with both her and the kids crying and begging me to stay. At the time, I could not explain the tremendous power that made me do this. And even now, I cannot put into words the tremendous pain it caused me to go through with this. I cried during the entire sixty-five-mile trip to Oklahoma City.

CHAPTER TEN

Starting a New Life

Shortly after I arrived in Oklahoma City to stay, Jeannie, Julie, their old Scotty dog, and I all moved into a rented condominium. Although I was very happy to be with Jeannie, my anxieties over the family I'd left behind continued to plague me. Delores put up one big fight after another over anything connected to our divorce; she did everything in her power to stop it from happening and caused me a never-ending problems. She didn't really think I was all that much until she didn't have me anymore, and then she wanted me back badly. My sleepless nights continued, accompanied by many tears. I also sought medical help for stomach ulcers and nerve problems. The ulcers got so bad that, for a time, all I could keep down was milk and milkshakes.

After a few months in the condo, Jeannie and I bought a brand-new house together in Mustang, a suburb of Oklahoma City. We were both still in the middle of the mandatory six-month waiting periods required for divorces in Oklahoma and Missouri, so we couldn't get married yet, but Jeannie signed all the paperwork as Jeannie Schmitz and nobody ever questioned anything. Once both of our divorces were finalized, Jeannie and I were married on May 31, 1977. We both wore western clothes and cowboy boots at the ceremony; this was the type of clothing we wore almost every day. Shortly after our wedding, I adopted Julie as my daughter.

My children lived with their mother most of the time in our old house in Weatherford, which I'd signed over to Delores specifically so she'd have a place to raise the kids. But I had custody of both Chris and Raquel every other weekend, and they'd come to stay with Jeannie, Julie, and me in our new home in Mustang. After a short initial period of adjustment, the three children learned to love each other. Both of the girls were glad to have a sister, and Julie has always thought that her big stepbrother Chris hung the moon.

I have never been able to initiate an out-of-body experience at will, and probably because of all the turmoil of a divorce and remarriage, this was a quiet period for me on the soul travel front. Although I had no metaphysical experiences during this period, both of my daughters did.

Julie, the younger of the two girls, would get off the school bus and be at home for a short time before Jeannie got home from work. Julie told us that several times when she came in the house alone, she would see an old woman lying on the couch in the den. We asked her if this old woman ever said anything, and the reply was always, "No, but she looks at me and smiles." We asked her where this woman would go when she left, and Julie said that she just sort of disappeared. We have always felt that this guardian angel was a motherly type of spirit from a previous lifetime watching over this child while she was alone.

My daughter Raquel told me about a nighttime experience in which she got out of bed to go to the bathroom. When trying to turn the doorknob, she couldn't get a grip on it to make it turn. Then her hand and arm went completely through the wooden door. This scared her so badly that she jumped back into bed and stayed there the rest of the night. From my experiences of passing through solid objects such as walls, I know she had to be in an out-of-body state when this unusual event occurred. I have asked her several times if she has experienced any similar occurrences, and her reply is always, "No, and I don't want to, because it is too scary."

CHAPTER ELEVEN

Boom and Bust

Initially, my new business was exclusively focused on selling trucks. Then one day in early 1977, a real-estate agent stopped by my office and asked me if I was familiar with a huge metal building north of the airport that had been designed as a deluxe truck and trailer dealership. When I told him I knew exactly the building he was talking about, he said I could get it at a steal of a price. I would've loved to have had this property, but common sense told me it had to be far, far out of my price range. The real-estate agent kept insisting otherwise, and he finally persuaded me to come see the building up close. It was 13,000 square feet and sported a beautiful showroom and a garage that could house six semi-trucks with trailers at the same time. From a business perspective, the location was great since it sat on a very busy road, and the property also included five acres of surrounding land.

The agent filled me in on the history of the builders and the businessman who had contracted them to build this property to his specifications. The builders had used their own money to fund the construction. The businessman had moved in and set up shop as soon as they were finished, but he had now been operating there for six months without ever paying the builders a cent. The builders were understandably fed up with this situation, and so they were about to kick the businessman out. The builders' misfortune could become my great fortune, the agent explained, because they were looking to sell the property at a bargain-basement price. But

One of my oil field trucks on the job.

even at the greatly reduced price they were offering, the loans I would've needed to take out to buy the place were still quite daunting. The builders, however, were so eager to sell that they even agreed to help me with the financing. This was way too good a deal to pass up, so I said yes, and this great big, beautiful building became the new headquarters for my business.

With the remarkable facility that had practically just fallen into my lap, I expanded my business beyond just truck sales into transportation services. The oil fields in Oklahoma and Texas were really booming at that time, so I focused my new business entirely on this industry, providing trucks to transport drilling rigs and other related equipment. My own business boomed in parallel with that of the drilling companies, and my company expanded enormously over a very short period of time. For several years in the late seventies and early eighties, I was actually operating two separate trucking companies with a total of 100 trucks and 120 employees. We were doing between six and seven million dollars' worth of business a year. It was highly stressful work knowing that I had to make $20,000 a day just to pay all my employee's salaries and keep my trucks running.

By this point, Jeannie was putting in a lot of time helping me out with running the business. She ran the office, did all the bookkeeping, and supervised a staff of at least a dozen women who helped her with the office's operations. So the business kept both of us very busy. We worked all the time when we should've been taking out more time to enjoy life. But of course there were some real upsides to the money that was rolling

Here I am, along with my family and a few friends, enjoying one of the perks of my very successful business years.

in. For example, I bought Jeannie a new red corvette for her birthday in 1980. We also bought a big motor home and a jet boat. And since I'd been licensed as a private pilot since 1965, I took this opportunity to buy a small plane for myself. Sadly, the business kept me so busy that I had no time to actually fly it.

Jeannie had developed a passion for horse riding, and I bought her a horse of her own in 1981. We paid for the horse to be kept on a horse farm that was about five miles from our home in the suburbs. Jeannie soon decided that she wanted more horses. She also wanted to have them all close at hand, not living on someone else's property. As a family, we needed more room in general and all three of us liked the country. So we sold our house in Mustang and bought a house on a fifteen-acre plot of land in the small community of Banner, not far outside of Oklahoma City. In addition to the several horses Jeannie now owned, we soon had chickens, ducks, guinea fowl, and Texas longhorn cattle on our property too.

Unfortunately, my business went quickly from boom to bust in the following year. A large bank based in Oklahoma City had made a lot of oil-field-related loans that went sour, and as a result, the bank failed and went into FDIC receivership in early 1982. New drilling in the Oklahoma oil fields—the bread and butter of my transportation business—completely shut down. For a while, every day when I went to the post office, I'd get another notice that one of my customers had gone bankrupt. Some of them were pretty large drilling companies, but with their previous heavy commitments to new drilling sites that were now completely shut down, they just couldn't go on. My two businesses were left with over two million dollars in accounts receivable that were now uncollectable.

In July 1982, some of my own creditors got together and had my business declared a case of involuntary bankruptcy. I lost my big building and all of the trucks, and that was the end of my business. Jeannie and I also lost most of our toys too, such as the airplane. We were actually pretty lucky to keep our house and the fifteen acres of land it sat on. But we had a very large mortgage to support—$4,000 a month—because we'd set it up to pay it off fast when the money was flowing in freely. Jeannie and I had to figure out a way to keep up those payments and also, of course, support our daughter Julie.

As soon as my business collapsed, I immediately started buying and selling used trucks. Because so many drillers had shut down so suddenly in Oklahoma, there was now little need in the state for the thousands of trucks that had previously serviced these companies. Many of these trucks were put up for sale, and because the market was so flooded with them, their prices plummeted. I took the opportunity to buy these trucks on the cheap and sell them at a profit in other regions of the country, where the truck markets were considerably healthier.

I did all right with this business, but I was still hard pressed to meet all my financial obligations with the profits I made. Fortunately, through previous connections I'd made in my now defunct business, I had the opportunity to lease a good deal of the acreage I owned to an oil business financier. He needed a lot of level land to store a number repossessed oil rigs, and the land I owned turned out to be perfect for him. He moved half a dozen rigs onto my property, and the amount he paid me for the use of my land helped me greatly in covering my mortgage payments.

CHAPTER TWELVE

My Soul Travels Resume

In the fall of 1982, my son Chris was preparing to start college at Baylor University in Waco, Texas. He had been living with his mother and sister some sixty miles away. He called and said he had been taking care of Honey, the old boxer dog that we had bought some nine or ten years before, but he couldn't take her to college with him and his mother no longer wanted the dog.

I had always had a very special love for this dog, and I think the feeling was mutual. I told Chris to bring her to my house so that I could take good care of her for the rest of her days. He brought Honey to my home on his way out of state to start college, and I put her inside a fenced yard. The people we bought our house from had kept three smaller dogs in that same yard, and so I assumed the fence was in good shape.

The next morning when I got out of bed, I discovered that Honey had broken some fence wires and gotten out through the hole she had created during the night. Her leather collar was lying near the fence but she was gone. I cried big tears because I loved her, and it had been my decision to leave her in the yard instead of in the house at night. Jeannie and I spent the next two days scouring the neighborhood, but we never found her. I blamed myself repeatedly for not taking better care of the beloved old dog, and I did not forgive myself.

As I indicated before, my soul travel experiences had not been very frequent or very exciting since around the time that I met Jeannie. In the

Honey, my old, beloved boxer.

first year or so, I believe that this was due to the anxieties associated with my divorce. Although those worries faded away over time, they were then replaced by the extreme pressures involved in running my two trucking companies. Doing that seemed to use up all the strength my body had during the workday. I not only had the stresses of my work draining my energy, but I also developed some serious intestinal issues around this time as well.

All my life, my soul travel experiences seemed to take an enormous amount of energy to endure, despite the fact that they often lasted no more than a minute or two at a time. The strength in my physical body was sapped by the problems I encountered in running this large business and my health issues, so there was none left in me at night for soul travel.

I have never had a clue as to why soul travel takes so much energy from my physical body, which always remains in bed in a sleep-like state. Talking with other experienced soul travelers and also reading everything that I could find on the subject, I still have no explanation. How can the physical body lose so much energy when the soul leaves it to travel around other planes and the heavens? There must be some type of connection between the two even during separation. Or maybe the soul tires while it's traveling and renews itself after returning back into the body, sharing the body's energy.

Whatever the case, in the years following the collapse of my transportation business, I suddenly had far less stress in my life. As I've mentioned, I did experience some financial struggles during this time, so it was hardly a time completely free of worry. But the pressures and anxieties I now faced took up far less of my time and energy than running my big business. As a result, my soul travels began to happen again. They started out slowly, much like my initial experiences as a teenager, with my soul rarely floating outside the boundaries of my own home.

Two years after I had lost my dog Honey, she appeared to me during one of my soul travel experiences. She looked middle-aged and in excellent health. I was surprised and very glad to see her standing five or six feet from me. She looked directly at me and said, "Stop blaming yourself. It was not your fault. I went through the fence because my time had come to move on. I am where I want to be and doing what I need to be doing." I moved toward her and bent down to pet her head but before I could touch her, she faded away.

I immediately returned to my body and awakened with mixed emotions. I shed tears of relief and joy, now that I finally knew Honey was all right. For the next few days, I had many thoughts about the experience. I didn't know where she was, but I knew it was a peaceful place with no pressures. I did not see any other beings around her nor did I travel through a long tunnel to meet her. This was the first times in my life that I realized animals have souls that live on forever, just as human souls do.

After thinking about this for a time, I told Jeannie that I would never pick up a gun and kill or harm an animal again. This went so far that I quit killing red ants in the yard and started using live traps to control mice. As the days went on, I developed a new respect for our pets and our horses. I found great joy in talking to them and looking deep into their eyes until it would seem that I could see their souls. I believe now that all of God's creatures were put on this planet for a purpose, and I do not have a right to disrupt their lives or harm them.

Of course, Jeannie understood this completely, especially given her love for horses. At this point, she and I had actually been saving for several years to construct a shelter for her to ride her horses under. The Western Oklahoma wind can chill you to the bone for half of the year and the hot sun can fry your brains during the other half. She needed a large roof with at least one wall to help break the wind.

We had bought some used metal and had saved enough money to have it erected into such a shelter. We hired a friend of mine who was in this type of business. As his crew started work, he told me we needed a concrete foundation and that it needed to be larger than we first planned.

After the foundation and the substructure was in place, he explained that our used metal would not work very well for the roof because it was so crooked there would be no way to keep rain from running through all the cracks. After installing new metal on the roof, he convinced me that we also needed new metal for the wall and that we really should put up four walls and have a nice enclosed building with a couple of big doors.

We had been paying for the material and labor as this building progressed, but now we were out of money. As the delivery trucks brought all of this expensive new metal, I started to worry about how we would be able to pay for it. A couple of weeks passed and the time to come up with more money was approaching very quickly. I was worrying about this pending problem as I went to bed one night.

During a soul travel experience later that night, I was told not to worry about the arena building and was assured that it would work out all right. I was not told how or when this might happen. In recounting this particular event to others, I have been asked who told me these things. I honestly cannot say; there was no being that I could see in front of me, and it wasn't really even like I was hearing spoken words with my ears. It felt more like a knowing that just came into my mind, but I feel sure that it was placed there by someone or something else; it was not a thought that originally came from within my own mind.

A couple of days passed and I started selling some old pieces of equipment that had been sitting in the weeds for seven or eight years. I had been trying to sell this equipment for quite some time, but this was the first time anyone had been interested in purchasing any of it for several years. People seemed to come out of nowhere, buying one or two pieces, until I had sold all of it in a very short period of time. Those sales created almost enough money to finish paying for all the supplies and labor, and so the building was finished.

CHAPTER THIRTEEN

Message from Grandpa

Another year or so passed before my next substantial spiritual experience, but it was a whopper. During the previous thirty years, I would leave my body slowly and float around close by, most of the time not going anywhere in particular. The only real exception to this was the experience of the tunnel and the white light that I described previously. Now I had my second soul travel experience that felt like a big trip rather than just floating around my home or my neighborhood.

I was in bed half asleep, lying on my stomach, when all of a sudden I flew out of my body with great force and started turning loops. My feet went up first and I turned one complete loop before going through the ceiling. I could feel a very strong pull, almost like a giant magnet was pulling me toward it. After several more feet-first loops above the house, I quit turning and was pulled in a straight line very quickly, or at least the rushing of air past me gave a sensation of great speed. Then all of a sudden, I stopped moving and found myself in a peaceful place, standing on my feet. I found that I was inside a huge room with off-white walls and a high ceiling. The structure had the look of concrete, but no windows or any color inside. I couldn't see any form of lighting in place anywhere, but somehow it was not very dark inside of this building.

As soon as I realized I was alone in a strange place, my grandpa on my mother's side of the family appeared to me. He was standing five or six feet from me and he appeared to be about fifty years old. He had died twenty years previous to this at the age of eighty-five. I remember thinking that this was how he looked when I was a little kid. He was dressed in the same type of pants and shirt as I remembered him wearing for many years. When he drove a motor grader on the county roads during the work week, he always wore bib overalls. But now he was wearing the clothes I remember him wearing on weekends—khaki trousers and a plaid shirt. It's hard to find the words to describe how it felt to be standing in front of him, twenty-five years after he had crossed over. He was just as much alive as I was, and he looked healthy and happy.

"Gene!" he called, "Go back and tell the ones who are worrying about me to quit their worrying. I am where I want to be and doing what I need to be doing. Go back and tell them to quit worrying." It was wonderful to hear his voice, but he gave his message in the tone of a strong command. I stepped toward him, trying to put my left arm around his shoulders to give him a hug and I tried to shake his hand with my right hand at the same time. Just as I was ready to feel the hug and the handshake, he drifted slowly away.

Needless to say, I made a quick return trip back to my body and sat up in bed wide awake. I was experiencing the same feelings I had when I had met Honey, my boxer dog, through soul travel. I didn't know where my grandpa was, but I did know that it was a peaceful place, and one that I didn't have to travel through any tunnels to reach. I spent the rest of the night awake with an elevated heart rate and heavy breathing. I remember thinking that this message he commanded me to deliver must be very important to him.

Then another realization hit me—my grandpa hadn't said to whom I should deliver his message. After Jeannie heard about this incredible experience, she asked, "Who are you going to tell?" After thinking about her question, I had to admit that I was scared to tell anyone. I had never heard of anyone else having this kind of contact and didn't want people thinking that I was completely crazy.

My mother is the oldest of seven children. Her youngest brother and only sister were born after she married and left home. That means I am close to the same age as my uncle and aunt. I had always known that my mother was particularly close to her father. Having lost her mother, she cared for him and her little sister by cooking meals and creating a warm, home-like atmosphere for them.

After much thought, I delivered my grandpa's message to my mother. She listened intently and cried. Looking back, I think this message was mainly for her, and I have always thought she was relieved to know her father was fine. He was a good man, but I don't remember him spending any time in a church house.

I also told one of my uncles and my aunt about their father's commands to stop worrying about him. My uncle seemed to accept the message well and even show some relief. However, my aunt said, "I have known you a long time and I've always thought you were a little crazy. Now I am sure of it."

I started thinking that maybe I could visit everybody in this mystical place and have a really great time, but this has never happened. It seems these experiences are not something that you can play around with and choose. Instead, they are allowed to happen to fulfill a real need to make someone more at peace with a particular situation. Evidently, it was very important for grandpa to give me his message.

I would like to have had a hug or felt a handshake from grandpa, but this was not allowed. It was almost exactly the same situation as when I bent down over the spirit of Honey, my old boxer, and she faded away. Just as my hands were ready to feel these old friends, they dissipated and were gone. I remember thinking aloud, "I wonder where my grandmother is?" She had crossed over twenty years before my grandfather did.

The more I thought back on this experience, the more honored I felt to have been chosen as a messenger to help grandpa get his message delivered back to his loved ones in the physical plane.

CHAPTER FOURTEEN

Angels and Animals

After the experience of meeting my grandpa, my soul travel seemed to get more frequent and have deeper meanings. I would often encounter many different beings, but never anyone I knew. Most of the time, it seemed that they were busy with their own thing and really didn't want me to bother them, although they were never unfriendly or unkind. I still had some scary feelings when I would first leave my body, but by now the travels were interesting enough to overcome the little bit of fear that remained in me. I was no longer afraid of getting lost and, at least up until this point, I had never encountered a bad situation. But knowing I had left my body behind and could pass through solid objects was so different than anything else in my life that I still had some lingering fear.

During this time period when I was outside working or tending to the animals on the place where we lived, I would see a flicker of something near me. I wear glasses and a beam of light will often reflect off the lens or the frames, sometimes causing me to think I'd seen something when I really hadn't. Realizing this, I kind of blew the flicker off and didn't give it much more thought for a while. This phenomenon would happen most often inside a huge horse-riding arena where my wife gave riding lessons to young people. When the flickers started happening much more frequently, I could no longer just ignore them. I would sometimes put my glasses in my shirt pocket for a time and it would still happen, so I knew it wasn't a reflection off the lenses or the frames.

Jeannie not only got a degree in equine sciences in the eighties, but she also became a competitive barrel rider.

Paying close attention for a couple of weeks, I finally told Jeannie that something was going to happen, but I didn't know whether it would be good or bad. She asked what I was talking about. I replied that I'd been seeing what I thought were angels around our place for the last two or three weeks. Jeannie asked me if they had wings or if it was something else about them that made me think they were angels. I hadn't seen any wings. I explained that these beings were about the same size as humans and had similarly shaped bodies. They were always at least five or six feet above the ground, and they were always moving in different directions from one another.

It was more a matter of feeling than anything I can explain logically that led me to believe these were angels. But I can at least point to a few specific details that suggest distinct differences between these beings and the souls I'd seen floating through my room in so many of my out-of-body experiences. I could always see those floating souls pretty clearly—enough to tell whether they were male or female, what color their hair was, and what type of clothing they were wearing. These beings I'm calling angels were much harder to see, and there was no way I could have made up these kinds of specific details with any of them.

Jeannie said she hadn't seen anything, but that she had experienced the strange feeling of a presence when she was giving riding lessons in the arena building. A couple of days after that, she'd just finished giving a lesson on the same old mare that she used with small children nearly every day. She was taking the saddle and the tack off of the old mare, which was just standing there half-asleep. All of a sudden, the mare jumped off the ground and snorted. Her eyes were larger than silver dollars and she acted as if she had just seen something that scared her a great deal. This was the only time the old horse had ever demonstrated such behavior.

I have heard many times that horses and cats have kind of a special gift that allows them to possibly contact or accept spiritual beings more easily than other animals. When the old mare's eyes got so big and she jumped and snorted, she must have seen one of the visiting angels that I have been talking about. Jeannie said that the mare was staring at one particular place during that whole incident. She never took her eyes off of that place during her period of panic. Then all of a sudden, she calmed down. Evidently she had seen an angel for a short time, and then that angel had left.

After this incident, my angel sightings stopped completely. Nothing new, different, good, or bad happened in our lives for quite some time, although my soul travels continued when I went to sleep at night. But in my waking life, I had no more sightings of what I thought were the angels, and Jeannie said that her previous sense of a presence in the horse arena was also gone.

CHAPTER FIFTEEN

New Traveling Companions

I could never cause a soul travel experience to happen or even predict when one would happen. Sometimes I would experience them several nights in a row, and then it might be three or four months before I'd have my next one.

It was at around this time that my soul travels took another interesting turn. Previously, I had always been alone in my travels. But now I began to notice that I often had a silent companion at my side, and sometimes I'd even have two of them. This was a new and completely different situation. I had to wonder who they were and who had sent them.

I had almost always already left my body and entered high-speed soul travel mode before I even realized these guides were with me. They would stay by my sides, back far enough that I could just barely see them. It seemed that they wanted me to pay attention to where we were going and think about what they were showing me instead of focusing on them. Whenever I would inquire who they were and what their intentions for me were, my guides either maintained a stony silence or told me that they weren't here to answer my questions.

Although I could feel these guides had an aura of goodness about them, they were definitely not overly friendly. I didn't understand why they we so formal in their actions, almost to the point of being cold. They were usually to my sides, almost in my peripheral vision, and somehow I could never really get a good look at their faces. From what little I could make out of their faces, I never recognized any of them. I'm not really sure if the same ones ever came back more than once, but I am sure that I had at least several different guides through the years.

I thought to myself, "Who am I to deserve such divine guidance and help from these guides or angels, whoever they were?" I knew I was a nobody in the great scheme of heaven and earth, and I had never spent any of my precious time going to church, doing missionary work, or really anything that might benefit my fellow man. I had spent a lot of time as an altar boy in the Catholic Church when I was younger, but the main reason I did that was because it let me get out of school for half a day without being counted absent.

I was always excited to have these guides along with me, because I knew whatever I would be shown was important to someone in the spiritual realm or they would not have sent these guys. I never understood why they never really talked to me or answered any of my questions or why they acted so cold toward me. It took a while for me to feel comfortable having these guys along with me during my soul travels, because they were so stern and cold and businesslike in their actions. If they would've just told me who sent them, I probably would've been elated to know that their big bosses even knew that I existed.

When I think back on my mysterious guides, I have to wonder if they were people I had known in my past incarnations. Is it possible that they owed me a karmic debt of some kind and were now choosing to pay it by taking the time to travel with me and show me different things? Maybe doing these things helped their own soul development. But how were they chosen to help me? Who made the decisions regarding who came down to get me and show me these things? It would certainly be interesting to know who they worked for or why they were the particular ones chosen for these tasks.

CHAPTER SIXTEEN

The Council of Twelve and Other Journeys with My Guides

The first trips I took with my new guides were journeys to places that seemed to me to be completely separate planes from the physical plane where I lived my normal life. Each plane seemed to be characterized by a different sound and usually a different color. Soft red, yellow, blue, brown, and pale green seemed to be the most prevalent colors. The sound of chimes, winds blowing gently, and many voices singing softly were some of the different things I heard while visiting these other planes.

Some of these planes I visited more than once, but the most memorable of them all I was only treated to once. On this plane, I heard the most beautiful music that I could imagine. It sounded as if a thousand bells were all playing at once; it was truly the greatest sound I have ever heard while in or out of my body.

Soon another very interesting travel ended in a strange but very real place. My travel companion and I wound up at a concrete building that we entered through a door. Assisted by my guide, I located a huge room within the building that contained a large table shaped like a half moon. Twelve men sat behind the table with their chairs arranged so that all twelve could see each other and all could see the front area equally well. I felt an instant and very strong sense of reverence and respect for these twelve elders, and I also got the sense that these were very powerful men. I realized that this was a special place and these were very special men.

I was brought into the center of the room, so that I stood in front of the half-moon-shaped table. All twelve men sat in their chairs looking at me. They were older men with auras of being very wise. I remember wondering who these beings were and what and who they had control over. I was not given any clues to help answer these questions. They were the only beings I have seen on the other side who appeared to be more than about fifty years old. These men looked more like they were in their eighties. They had white hair, aged faces, and facial hair. Each one looked distinctly different than the rest, but all were dressed in robes of subdued neutral colors and other clothing that suggested Biblical times. They all appeared to have skin that ranged from olive to white. They did not appear to be of Middle Eastern origin but instead more closely resembled the Anglo-Saxon elders of my own past.

These men spoke without moving their lips. I followed their eyes and understood a little of what they said, but most of it was beyond my comprehension. They were communicating with each other, leaning toward each other as if to talk, but still their lips did not move. As I stood there, one of the men near the center of the table stood up and asked my guide, "Is this the guy you told us about?" It was a little surprising to hear such informal language come from this very serious elder. My guide, who was standing at my right side, responded that I was indeed the man in question. The elder then said, "No, we do not want him at this time. He is too young and he is not ready yet." This elder never actually looked at me during this exchange—his focus seemed to be completely directed toward my guide.

Not being wanted by this council of elders yet didn't bother me much, but I wondered what they were talking about and what they might eventually want me for. I was escorted out of the room, and then my soul returned to my body. Many years have passed since this happened and I still don't know what these twelve men represent.

Soon after this meeting, I had another soul-travel experience in which I arrived near a low, windowless building that was extremely long in its design. I noticed that it was darker in color than the ones I had been inside of on previous soul travels. I also remember thinking it was the oldest looking building I'd seen during any of my soul travels, and yet it also seemed less used than the others I had seen. I had no idea what the building might have been used for, but I sensed that it was unoccupied. Perhaps it was used for some kind of storage?

Walking closer to the building, I heard several sounds coming from the other side. I thought I could hear someone speaking, or maybe it was several people speaking at the same time. I thought I would go around to the other side and see what was happening. I looked toward one end of the very long building and thought it would be a long way to walk. I then looked in the other direction and decided it would also be a very long way to walk around this end too.

I don't know why, but the thought came to me that I just might be able to fly over the top of the wall separating the two halves of the building. Almost as soon as I had this thought, I found myself jumping over the wall and then landing on the ground on the other side, standing on my feet. This side of the building looked the same as the other, and looking around, I didn't see anyone. I was disappointed because I expected to find someone talking and doing something to cause the noise I had heard, but again I found myself all alone. I then returned to my body, ending this experience.

In another out-of-body experience around the same time, I traveled with one guide at very fast speeds for what seemed a long distance. We finally came to a neighborhood that was completely strange to me. We slowly walked up the middle of a street with wooden houses on both sides. The houses were all built alike and painted white. As I walked, I noticed the street surface was a hard material that I could not identify. It was not concrete, stone, asphalt, or brick. At first I thought maybe it was extremely hard-packed soil. After a closer look, I decided it was not soil either.

This street was built on a gently sloping hill, and as I walked uphill along it, I noticed that each house was a little bit higher than the previous one. These houses were well kept, and although I didn't see any of the inhabitants, I could tell that these homes were all lived in. I noticed that there were no driveways or garages, and this fact made me think that automobiles were not used for transportation here. I wish that I knew where this place was located or how I could go back there for another visit. If I had to make a guess, I would venture that it is on a different plane than the physical one we live in. There has to be a reason I was shown this neighborhood where everyone lives on exactly the same social level, no one having anything bigger or fancier than any of their neighbors.

CHAPTER SEVENTEEN

Life on Other Planets

As I mentioned before, I usually wasn't aware of the presence of my guides until well after I'd left my body and entered the high-speed soul travel mode. There was only one time that my guides ever appeared to me in my bedroom, at the very start of my out-of-body experience. This was the beginning of the longest soul travel experience that I can ever remember having.

I was floating above my sleeping body when my guides appeared. I could see them a little better than usual, although I still couldn't really make out their faces very well. I took this unique opportunity to ask my guides where they were taking me and what we were going to do when we got there. As usual, I got no answers. Of course, I was also curious about who was behind the trips I was being taken on, and what they wanted me to get out of these experiences. So I asked my guides, "Who are you guys and who do you work for? Who sent you after me? Who's your boss—is it Jesus, Michael the Archangel, or someone else?" This was the first time I had ever bucked up against my guides even a little bit.

One of my guides responded in typical fashion, "We were sent to do a job. We are not here to answer any questions or visit. Now let's go." And then I felt both of my guides kind of nudge me on the back of my shoulders and we started moving into high-speed travel mode. I had a guide on each side of me, and we traveled in an upright position as if we were walking. The sound of passing through rushing air was very prevalent, as was the sensation of moving as fast as a bullet. The sensation lasted a long time and it was easy to tell we were traveling a great distance.

This was the only time that I ever put up any resistance to any of the guides that accompanied me on my soul travels, but I gained nothing from my boldness. I hadn't received a single hint as to who they were or who had sent them. I thought surely I was not important enough for someone in high command to send two helpers out to carry out a mission. I have to wonder, though, what might have happened if I had refused to go with my guides when they came to get me. Did they possess some kind of power they could've used to make me go against my will? Or would they have simply scratched me off the list, so to speak, and forgotten about me in the future? They might've simply said, "Okay, fellow, you can muddle through several hundred more incarnations and try to learn what you need to know on your own. You won't get any more help from us."

I got a stronger-than-usual sense that it was very important for these two guides to show me whatever it was that we were heading toward on this particular trip. After a time, our speed of travel slowed, and instead of moving in a straight line, we began to circle. I soon realized we were above a large sphere similar to our Earth. We circled completely around what I think was a planet and continued to travel in another straight line. After just a short time, we circled a second planet much the same as the first. As I was looking down at this second planet, one of my guides told me that I needed to be shown that there is life in faraway places that the people of Earth do not know about.

I remember these planets looking a lot like the Earth does in pictures taken from space. There were several different colors on the surface, each one letting me know there was life of some form. The second planet we circled looked very similar to the first, but it was not a carbon copy. I felt like this second one was somewhat smaller in size. Although I was much too high above the surface to see anyone, I had the strong sense that these two planets were indeed inhabited. I remember the return trip to my body being extremely long, and I also moving at what seemed to be tremendous speeds.

I certainly don't remember ever seeing a UFO or having any contact with an alien being, and I've never spent any time studying life on other planets. But for some reason, my two guides thought it was very important to show me these two faraway planets. After one of them told me that I needed to know that there is life in faraway places that I didn't even know existed, I feel certain that there's an abundance of life in many places besides planet Earth.

As far as I know, I've never seen any extraterrestrial beings, but if I ever do, I'm going to welcome them with open arms. I know that there is only one Supreme Being, the one that we call God. This makes all of us—including extraterrestrials—spiritual brothers and sisters who all come from one Creator. If I am ever blessed to make contact with visitors from another planet, I'm going to beg for a ride in their spaceship. I think that would be supercool.

CHAPTER EIGHTEEN

Meeting Willie

While reading the paper, Jeannie saw an ad for a psychic fair that was coming to town the following weekend. We attended it on Sunday afternoon, and this was my first time to be around anyone who would even say the word "psychic," let alone be willing to share unexplained experiences.

Although I did not participate in any discussions or group activities, I was intrigued by a young Native American named Willie who would put himself into a trance-like state to do psychic readings for people. Picking up one of his business cards, I learned that he would do personal readings in which he looked into the future for a small fee. I had heard of fortune-tellers before, but I thought they were all older women with funny clothes and strange accents, sitting in a dark room with lots of beads hanging everywhere, looking into crystal balls. I was surprised to see this young man dressed the same way I was, sitting doing readings in broad daylight with enough noise going on around him that it was difficult to talk to anyone.

A week later, I called Willie and set up a time for him to come to my house and do a reading for me. When he told me the small fee he would charge, I thought that the amount would hardly pay for the gas his car would burn coming to my house. The amount he charged would not even match the minimum hourly wage standard for that time, so I knew his reasons for doing this service couldn't be motivated by profit. I was excited, but not really because I wanted to know my future so badly—I actually felt like that could be scary. I was more excited by the prospect of sharing some of my own out-of-body experiences with Willie.

When he arrived, he was wearing the same baseball cap he had worn at the psychic fair. After a couple of minutes of visiting, he learned that I did not feel prejudiced against Native Americans and that I in fact had a lot of admiration for them. This led him to taking the ball cap off and letting his long brown hair fall to his shoulders.

Willie asked that I clear my mind and remain quiet to give him a chance to communicate with higher powers. I remember thinking that he probably could get information from a higher source than I had yet tapped in my own soul travels. Clutching a rock in his left hand, Willie put himself in a trance-like state and began talking slowly, saying that I was an old soul who had experienced many different incarnations and learned many lessons through the ages. He also said my health was good and that I would continue to live and work in the same place for several more years. I asked a couple of questions that he only answered in a very vague fashion.

After Willie came out of the trance, I asked about the rock he was holding. He replied that it was a gift from a good friend and it helped to make his psychic abilities stronger. My next question was, "How did you learn to do that?" His reply was that his father and mother could both heal and they had taught him all of his life that he could heal and see both forward and backward in time. When he mentioned being able to see into the past, he got my full attention. I was a lot more interested in who I had been and where I had lived in past lives than I was in what would happen to me in the future.

I thought that this young man was truly blessed to have such an outstanding talent. I had always heard that Native Americans had learned to live in better harmony with Mother Nature and the Earth than most of the rest of us. Since this was the first psychic look into my future I'd received, it had quite an impact on me. It gave me the idea that I would live for a long time and that I would be able to survive the financial problems that I was experiencing again at this point in my life. This helped me to have new hope for the future and gave me newfound strength to try harder with each passing day.

CHAPTER NINETEEN

Meditation Sessions at the Crystal Healing Center

Willie invited me to come to a meditation meeting on Tuesday evenings at a place he called the Crystal Healing Center. He said there was no charge, but we could make a small love offering if we desired; it would help to pay the rent. These meetings turned out to be refreshing experiences where my wife and I would participate with others while Willie led us in group meditation. Sometimes the crowd would be a total of five or six, and sometimes as many as a dozen people. The participants ranged from teenagers to retired persons from every walk of life. I was relieved to find that this was not a group of weirdoes and that each member of the group was a good person who was working to care for a family.

I very much looked forward to these Tuesday evening sessions. Being in the presence of several people that understood and were interested in my soul travel stories made me feel extremely comfortable. I had been keeping these experiences to myself for thirty years with the exception of three or four family members. I knew that if I said anything about this to most people, they would think I was at least half out of my mind.

Other than Willie, I don't remember anyone in this group talking about soul travel experiences, but they were all interested in learning about heaven and Earth and what their souls might encounter after their brief physical lives on planet Earth. They each had different stories to share, all of which were very interesting. We would end these sessions with a group meditation and a chance for each of us to share what we might have learned or experienced during the meditation that evening.

Although I enjoyed these sessions, I had a hard time getting my mind to stop thinking about the day's events or worrying about the next day's upcoming problems. Before one session, Willie handed me the rock that he usually held himself and said, "Hold this and see if it helps." Part of the rock was transparent enough that you could see light through it, but it looked cloudy. Willie explained that a person's receiving hand is the one opposite his or her predominant side. Since I am right-handed, that meant I should hold the rock in my left hand. As I wrapped the fingers of my left hand around the rock, I noticed that it felt cold.

After the meditation, I thought that the rock hadn't helped much if at all, but I did notice that it felt hot in my hand. I asked Willie how it could get hotter than my body temperature. He felt its warmth and passed it through the crowd for others to feel. Everyone agreed it was hot to the touch.

In further sessions, I finally learned to slow down my mind somewhat and started to feel what meditating was like. Each time I would hold Willie's rock and each time it would become hot. No one knew how it could get so much warmer than my body temperature, but Willie would often say that he thought his rock liked me.

I seemed to be having more trouble than most of the others in the group keeping my mind clear and concentrating on the meditations. After a meeting, Willie said, "I want you to take this rock home with you and hold it every day as you try to practice your meditation." After doing this for a week, I was not sure that the rock had really helped me in my meditations. But when I returned the rock to Willie at the next meeting, he looked at it with much excitement and said, "Look, the rock is clear, I can see through it. The cloudiness is gone." Sure enough, there was quite a difference in its clarity. Willie said, "Now I know the rock likes you."

Because it was extremely hard for me to meditate, most of the time I usually just relaxed and listened to Willie's soft voice while the other group members meditated more successfully than I could ever manage. Unfortunately, I never got my mind to slow down enough to enter any type of meditation. One particular time, I was sitting in a large recliner chair during a session, and I was feeling very relaxed. The next thing I remember was that Willie and Jeannie were standing over me with extremely worried looks on their faces. Looking at others in the room, I noticed that they also looked as if they had just seen a man return from the dead. It took several minutes before I could get out of the chair. I was confused and my mind seemed like it was fuzzy, as if I was still half-asleep. I could tell by the look on Willie's face that whatever had happened was quite a shock to him. He was quite bewildered by it.

After some time passed, I could see, hear, and think more clearly. I was told that when Willie was ready to bring the meditation period to an end, he had asked that everyone return to their bodies and awake in their normal positions they had been occupying before the meditation. This is the same thing he would do every time he brought the group out of a meditation. But this time, everyone returned awake and alert except me. Everyone became worried when Willie tried to waken me several times without results. Willie said that he had never been unable to bring someone out of deep meditation before.

Later, Jeannie said that she was scared when she saw how worried Willie was as he stood over me, trying everything he knew to bring me back to consciousness. She said she was afraid maybe my soul had gone somewhere and decided not to return. She said my body was perfectly still with no signs of life and my coloring was a pale white. At the time, I had no memory of where I had ventured or what I might have been doing. I've thought about this experience many times in the following years, and I still don't remember anything else about the session.

CHAPTER TWENTY

Animal Guides

Willie explained that the Native Americans believe that we have animal guides as well as human-type guardian angel guides. He said if the group wanted, he would try to call up our animal guides at the next meeting. This meeting proved very interesting. Willie started by telling us that to call the animals out of the forest, he used Native American language because he didn't know how to call them out using English words. He explained that all the animals would come out to the edge of the forest, and we could go up to them, talk to them, and play with them. He said after a short time, the animals would all leave except for our individual guides.

Each person took a turn in telling the group about his or her newfound guide. Jeannie explained that her guide was a horse of a deep, dark-red color. She said this horse stayed by her and she petted him affectionately. The fact that Jeannie's guide was a horse was no surprise to me, because she dearly loved horses and had become an accomplished rider and barrel racer by this time.

After each group member except for me had described his or her own animal guide, Willie told me to look down at the coyote lying at my feet. I tried to see this coyote but couldn't, no matter how hard I looked. After the meditation ended, I enjoyed listening to everyone else's experiences, including my wife's. Jeannie explained that this time she had ridden her horse at great speeds across what seemed to be flattop mesas. She said it had been a very exciting experience and she could hardly wait to try this ride again. When my turn came, I had to say again that all I could see was darkness.

Willie said that he could now see that I had two animal guides, the coyote by my feet, and an eagle above my shoulder. I asked him why I might have two different ones and he said the coyote helped to guide my earthly travels and the eagle had the ability to fly high and help me see over distant horizons.

Jeannie had marvelous experiences with her new horse guide over several more meditation sessions. On one ride, she was able to see through her horse's eyes as they rode like the wind, moving from the top of one mesa to the top of another distant one with the greatest of ease. She said that a horse can focus on distance with his left eye to spot any danger while using his right eye to focus on the grass that it is eating. She also noted that the horse's range of vision is so wide that he can almost see behind him without turning his head. She had even learned that her horse guide's name was Orion.

Most of the other members had similar wonderful experiences to share each week except me. It seemed that the harder I tried to see my coyote or my eagle, the more frustrated I became. Willie told me to just relax at the next session; he said that I was probably just trying too hard.

After a couple more tries, I had one of the most memorable experiences of my entire life—well, this lifetime anyway. While I was trying hard to see one of my animal guides, I suddenly realized I was actually flying above a river. I could see small objects on the ground, even though I could also tell that the ground was several hundred feet below me. It took me a minute or so to realize I had become a part of my eagle. I was seeing through its eyes and gliding on the warm air currents that I could feel coming up from the ground. As I've mentioned before, I had been a private pilot for a number of years at this point and loved to fly small planes. However, this sensation of gliding through the wind with almost no effort was a grand feeling, much neater than being in an airplane.

I was soaring above a vast area with mountains nearby and many flat-topped mesas in the distance. A large river with many bends wound its way along the landscape, flowing around and through the hills. As I was enjoying the incredible ability to see much farther than I had ever been able to see before, I also realized that I would sometimes have to flap my wings to gain altitude and keep from coming too close to the ground. It seemed that five or six good wing flaps would propel me to much higher altitudes, and then I would just turn from side to side and glide for a long time. I remember thinking that these newfound wings seemed big compared to the rest of me and that flapping them took quite a bit of effort.

This flying was a most pleasant experience and gave me the fantastic feeling of being totally free, gliding through the air, feeling the warm air currents underneath pushing me upward. Being able to see a mouse running through the grass on the riverbank from several hundred feet above the water was incredible. When I would start sinking toward the ground, three or four flaps of my huge wings would bring back my altitude quickly. I was amazed at the amount of strength it took to flap these wings, though. It was truly hard work—like running at top speed in my human body. Several flaps in a row would be tiring, but then I could go back to the very enjoyable gliding experience and just relish the free feeling of flight again. I don't remember encountering any other flying birds during this experience.

When the meditation was over, I had a great story to tell. The experience was so real that it never crossed my mind that my story might be hard to believe, for I had just lived it and was very excited. When telling my story, I realized I had never actually seen this eagle since I had actually *become* the eagle.

When I asked Willie how this could possibly be, he said his father would tell a story about his uncle being able to outrun their old Ford car when they drove it from the farm where they lived to town several miles down dirt roads. When the family would get loaded in the car ready to travel, the uncle would say, "I will be in town before you guys get there." The children were told not to watch as the uncle ran behind the car as it started down the road, but that only made them more curious. Willie's father said that on one such occasion, he peeked and saw his uncle run until he came to a gate in the pasture fence. His uncle then laid down, rolled under the gate, and transformed into a coyote, which then ran very quickly across the pasture. Each time when this race took place, Willie's father's family would arrive in town in their car only to find their uncle standing there waiting for them.

The next morning, I woke up to another big surprise. My arms and my chest were so sore that I could hardly move. Both arms hurt, but the middle part of my chest hurt even worse. I could hardly pick up a coffee cup. This soreness stayed with me through two more days and was very uncomfortable. When I told Willie about my problems moving my arms, he said he knew of a much younger man than I who had experienced this same condition after flying as an eagle. This was the only time I ever experienced being an eagle, which was very disappointing since it had been enjoyable and so different than anything else I'd ever known in my life.

Soon after my flight as an eagle, I was finally able to see my coyote guide's face. It was a very small face, only about half as big as the coyotes I was used to seeing all my life. Ever since this experience, each time I see a half-grown coyote dead on the roadside, my heart breaks because I always think of my guide.

After this, I questioned several Native Americans about their knowledge of humans who had the ability to shapeshift into animals. Some of them had heard their tribe elders or medicine men mention it, but most didn't know what I was talking about. I have never made contact with anyone else who has had a shapeshifting experience like I had with the eagle or like Jeannie had with her horse guide.

I got the same type of responses when I questioned Native Americans about their animal guides. Most would say they had heard some talk of animal guides but had no personal experiences with them. Some of them would say, "No, I don't even know what you're talking about." However, I questioned one Native American man whose eyes lit up. "How do you know about animal guides?" he asked in obvious excitement. "White people are not supposed to know." He concluded that I must still have close ties to a tribe that I had been a part of in a previous incarnation.

CHAPTER TWENTY-ONE

Soul Crossings

Willie also did what he called a reading of soul crossings for Jeannie and me. He explained that he would look at all the past lifetimes of both of our souls and see when they crossed each other. Wherever such an intersection happened, it would indicate previous incarnations that my wife and I had spent together. Willie also said that souls will often reincarnate into a circle of family, friends, or acquaintances to fulfill their need to return good deeds rendered in a past life. On the other hand, they may do so to make right on harmful actions from the past. This circle will grow in size over the course of many incarnations as a soul evolves and works its way toward higher planes of existence.

Willie held both of our hands and entered a trance-like state. He said Jeannie and I had lived many lives together in the past. This past attachment to one another must be why we experienced love at first sight in this present lifetime. Willie told us that our last life as a couple was in the area of Boston before it was called Boston, and that we had been Quakers. "Now I know why you always wear a hat," Willie told me. "I see you wearing a big black hat and all black clothing in this past life. The two of you are doing a dance in the middle of the floor and a crowd of onlookers is sitting around the walls. Some of the crowd is whispering something. They are saying, 'It is not proper. It is not proper.' The reason for this is that when you two are dancing toward each other, you are rocking your hands forward and backward, forward and backward, but you are touching hands when you rock forward and this is considered improper behavior."

Willie went on to say, "You are speaking in English, but it sounds much different than we now speak. The words are very heavy and they sound very guttural. I am going to try to say some of those words." But after several tries, Willie gave up and said he just could not make these sounds.

Willie also did soul crossings for my son and me and then for Jeannie and her very close friend Polly. For both pairings, he was able to give us details on multiple lifetimes that we had spent together. When Willie did the soul crossing for Jeannie and Polly, he said that their souls had crossed so many times that he couldn't even count all of the instances.

Willie saw the last shared lifetime for Jeannie and her friend prior to the present-day one was in the very early twentieth century, when they were brothers named Jake and Jeremy. Jeannie was the younger of the two and looked up to the older brother, who was the dreamer of the family. Jeannie said that she was able to see along with Willie into this lifetime. She could even see what she wore—she described a specific cap, shirt, and pair of pants. She also described for me in detail what her big brother looked like and said that she thought he hung the moon.

The lifetime before that for them was in Europe. They were close friends but not related by blood. They were involved in a fight for freedom and one of them was killed. In another lifetime, they were again brothers, but this time they were merchants by trade and argumentative by nature. Arguing seemed to be their basic form of communication. Due to their dark skin and the surroundings they were in, Willie thought that this lifetime took place in Greece.

Further back in time, they were sisters in England. This time, Polly was the one who was able to see back into their previous shared lifetime. The girls were twins and their family was well-to-do. They were the daughters of Lord Dagmont. They wore fine silks and dresses, but they had a lonely existence. Other than the servants, they had only each other for company. Polly said that she could actually feel the cold through her robes and the soles of her shoes as she and her sister walked outside. She said their home seemed cold and drafty in spite of the huge fires in the fireplaces. She felt that this was a time that was very hard for people no matter what their economic station.

Another life took place in Egypt, with Jeannie and Polly as a mother and daughter. Both were servants. The daughter was very rebellious and the mother constantly tried to keep that rebellion in check. Their relationship as mother and daughter was kept a secret from everyone else for safety's sake.

In the time of Atlantis, there was no family relationship between Jeannie and Polly, but they were close friends and colleagues. Both were doctors. In this lifetime, the girls were extremely intelligent. They spent their time charting star systems and diagramming the ocean floor. This was the major reason for the soul connection. The two were so highly developed for that time that they only had each other to communicate with. No one else was interested in or could understand their work. This was one of their most powerful lifetimes, the one in which the love and respect of their two souls began. It became the basis for their souls returning in corresponding lifetimes throughout the centuries. In their present lives, there have been times when Jeannie and Polly seemed to communicate without words. When they are talking, one starts a sentence and the other finishes it without missing a beat.

When Willie did the soul crossing for me and my son, he said that we had been together in many past lives, more times than there are cards in a deck. The last lifetime he saw was where Boston is now located. My son was my uncle and he had come over to the New World first. He then worked hard and saved the money to pay my passage from the old country. Willie also saw us in another lifetime, working together on a sailing ship. One of us was the foreman and the other complained about a hard job he was given to do.

After thinking about the previous life in Boston, I realize that in the present lifetime, it had been my turn to work hard and earn money to raise and educate my son. This was a nice payback for his help in bringing me to this country in our last incarnation together.

CHAPTER TWENTY-TWO

A Mysterious Lecture and the End of Our Meditation Sessions

After we had been participating in meditation sessions at the Crystal Healing Center for close to a year, Jeannie was having her nails done one afternoon at a salon by a woman named Robin. When Robin asked Jeannie if she had been doing anything interesting lately, Jeannie told her about the meditation sessions. Robin was fascinated by this and said that she wanted to come to next week's session. Robin explained to Jeannie that she remembered being in her mother's womb before birth and could also remember making the decision to stay in this body and live out this incarnation at the age of two.

At the next meeting, I heard a young girl's voice at the door asking for Jeannie. I was sitting in a different room and I could not see the front door, but I heard my wife tell Robin to come in and meet me. When they walked around the corner where I was sitting, Robin saw me and said, "Oh! I know him. Just last week I saw him giving a psychic lecture to a large crowd of people." Although it felt as if Robin was an old friend, I know for sure we had never met on this physical plane before. I have also never given any type of a lecture of any sort in the physical realm. So when Robin saw my lecture, I must have been on a spiritual plane, having a soul-travel experience. She also had to be out-of-body to have been in the same place and on the same plane that I was.

I couldn't understand how I could have given a whole lecture during one of my soul travels and have no memory of any part of it. But many times when I returned to my body from a soul-travel experience, it would seem as if I'd been gone a long time, even though I could remember no more than a few seconds of it. This situation has troubled me somewhat in the past. I could never figure out this feeling of substantial time passing during which I can't remember where I might have been or what I might have experienced. Maybe I really was gone a long time, but could only remember just a few seconds of the journey.

Robin was a very interesting young woman to visit with since her childhood memories went back before birth and she also said she could always understand what people around her were thinking. This might explain why she was over twenty-five years old and still single, even though she was exceptionally pretty and had a great personality. Jeannie would tell her that she was going to have to lighten up a little and quit telling her boyfriends what they were thinking. It was just too much for them to handle!

It was at another session not long after this that Willie took out a book entitled *The Mysteries of Sedona* by Tom Dongo that he proceeded to share with our meditation group. The book told of strange centers of power called vortexes and explained that many of these vortexes were concentrated in an area around the small Arizona town of Sedona. After studying the pages of this very interesting book, we all wanted to go there and experience it for ourselves. Willie had not been out of his home state very much, but he soon headed for Sedona. When he returned a couple weeks later, we were all anxious to hear his stories.

Willie had chosen to hike into Boynton Canyon because the book said this area had strong ties to ancient Native American tribes. Willie finally arrived at a place in the canyon that felt right. He then settled down into a deep meditation in which his guides told him that he was a true shaman healer, but his Native tribe needed him more badly than the people in the big city. He said he had started making plans to close the Crystal Healing Center and return to his tribe some ninety miles away. Our group was troubled by this, for it meant an end to our great meditation sessions and presumably our contact with our animal guides.

Soon the Crystal Healing Center closed. Jeannie and I dearly missed having a place to go and join in a group meditation. We soon lost all contact with everyone from the group, including Willie. This all happened twenty years ago, and I have not had any contact with my coyote or my eagle since then. Jeannie, however, was able to contact her horse guide several times after Willie left. I can't recall many specific details about what she told me of these later encounters, but they occurred while Jeannie was meditating on her own, while she was sleeping, or both.

CHAPTER TWENTY-THREE

Out-of-Body Encounters with Evil

It was around this time that I had the only two negative encounters I ever experienced while visiting unknown planes during my soul travel experiences. At the outset of the first of these, I was in the middle of an out-of-body trip when I could tell that a dark force was coming toward me. Several other spirits had been floating near me, and they suddenly started moving away. I realized a strong spirit was getting nearer and nearer, until it actually came close enough to try to talk to me. Somehow, despite its nearness, I couldn't see this being well enough to make out the details of what it looked like, but I could certainly feel a very strong negativity surrounding it. I knew that I didn't want any part of this evil feeling, so I left and quickly returned to my body, ending the experience abruptly.

This was scary, for it was the first time I had encountered anything except love and total acceptance while in an out-of-body situation. My second face-to-face meeting with a dark force happened about a year later, and it was much more intense. I found myself in the presence of a very evil force—much more evil than the presence I had felt in the first experience. It seemed to be more than a single spirit; perhaps several spirits had combined into one force. I could see that it was quite dark and feel that it was very powerful as it approached me.

I started backing away to put some distance between myself and this evil being. As I was retreating, the force surrounded me like a strong whirlwind. It kept circling around and around me like it was trying to engulf me completely. I felt as if I had been trapped in the center of a tornado. The eerie feeling of evil increased, and I thought this force either intended to destroy me or take me into its very being.

I knew of only one escape and that was to leave this spiritual plane immediately and return to my body. But as I started the return trip, the evil followed me. This was the first time I had been followed by any spirit as I left another plane to return to my body. Even when guides were by my side showing me something, they would leave when I started my return trip.

This evil followed me to the physical plane and manifested itself as a hideous-looking creature. Fortunately, it did not manifest itself in my bedroom, but instead near an auxiliary building that was adjacent to my house. Although it looked more like a beast than a man, it stood on its hind legs and was well over six feet tall. Instead of feet, it had hooves that were split down the middle like a cow's. It had the face of a monster unlike anything I had ever seen. There was brown hair covering the head and body, but it had some type of cloth wrapped around its middle. Extreme evil radiated from this beast in all directions. Its face was so hideous that it was hard to look at, but I was scared to look away because I felt that if I did, I might possibly be engulfed by this thing, whatever it was.

I knew I had to do something; I was afraid it might go into the house where Jeannie was sleeping. I kept saying, "God made me, God made you, and he is more powerful than you are. I am part of God and I am a child of the light, so you cannot harm me." I kept saying this over and over. I was very scared, and it was taking all the energy I had to keep repeating the phrase. The evil beast stood its ground and didn't retreat, but it did not come any closer to me either.

It was hard, but I kept looking into that monstrous face and repeating the phrase as quickly and as loudly as I could. I had the strong sense that it didn't want to kill me physically or spiritually but rather that it wanted to make me a slave to help it recruit others to its evil ways. I also remember feeling that death would be much better than a life of slavery with this evil thing for a master.

I thought I was not making any progress because the beast never moved or showed signs of weakening in its desire to totally encompass me. I kept repeating my statement of faith until this evil being suddenly exploded into what must have been millions of pieces as small as dust particles. It was as if a bomb had gone off inside of this creature. For a few moments following the explosion, it looked like a cloud of fine dust disappearing into the air.

I knew the all-loving goodness from the white light had prevailed, and I was very thankful that I had been given enough faith to keep testifying that I was a child of the light and the supreme, all-powerful Creator. This encounter was the scariest I have ever experienced in this lifetime. I now pray each and every day, thanking God for the strong faith he gave me. But I also ask, "Please don't test me to that extreme again." I truly don't know if I would be strong enough to resist such a powerful dark force the next time. I hope I don't have to find out.

This ordeal made such an impression on me that I would never again go near the spot where the monster stood. Two years later, we sold our home in Banner and the surrounding fifteen acres of land. I have visited this property a number of times since selling it, but I always walk or drive around the specific area where the dark force manifested itself and stood upright like a man. Although I could never see any markings on the ground where the explosion took place before my eyes, I know that the evil beast was destroyed and didn't simply dissipate or disappear. I feel the all-loving white light took the time and effort to show me it is all-powerful, even when put up against the worst of evil and that it has enough love to protect each of us if we only have faith and don't give in to dark forces.

I have made the statement several times that there is nothing on this entire planet that could scare me as much as this experience. I would rather be charged by a vicious, wild animal or dropped off at midnight in an alleyway in the worst ghetto in a huge city. I think it would be much easier to face a wild animal or any number of human beings than it was to face this evil force.

CHAPTER TWENTY-FOUR

In Two Places at One Time

In the eighties, I had become acquainted with a man from Sacramento, California, named Charles. Our meeting started out as a business deal, but gradually we also became personal friends as time went on. He lived on a large ranch and each time he would tell me about his home, I wanted to visit his place more and more. As of this writing, however, I have still never made it to Sacramento.

One fall evening in the early nineties, I was watching the evening news. An expert explained that there would be a total eclipse of the moon during the night and it would be visible from where I lived in Oklahoma. I told Jeannie that it would be neat to see the eclipse, but that I was much too tired to stay up late, and so we both went to bed.

The next morning Charles called and asked where I was during the previous night. He asked if I had seen the lunar eclipse, and I told him I had slept through it. Charles said that he had made a new lady friend, Laurie Ann, and that they walked to a hillside on the ranch to watch this rare sight. He said as they sat on the grassy slope during the eclipse, he looked down the hill from where they sat and there I stood. Although Charles was flabbergasted, he said both he and Laurie Ann saw me standing there with my cowboy hat on. He said the experience was rather eerie—I didn't stay long and then I just sort of faded away. I had no recollection of leaving my body that night or seeing my friend on a grassy hillside in California.

A few months later, Charles and Laurie Ann came to Oklahoma on a business deal and stopped by my house. After introducing Laurie Ann to me and my wife, he asked her if I was the guy they had both seen on the night of the eclipse of the moon. She looked me over and replied, "Yes, he is the person." I hope to travel to Charles' ranch one day and visit this same hillside to see if anything looks familiar.

After we discussed how spiritual this experience had been, Charles shared another strange event that had happened to him about five years earlier. At the time, he was driving an eighteen-wheeler, hauling freight across the U.S. He hated his job and also was experiencing a tremendous amount of turmoil in his personal life. At the time, he couldn't even see much hope for any future improvement in his life. He said that suicide was heavily on his mind every day during this period. On one West Coast run, he had been talking on the CB radio to a driver who was hauling food in a refrigerated trailer. Charles didn't know this driver's real name, but he went by the CB handle of "Turkey Tracks."

Charles and Turkey Tracks met up at a truck stop in Ontario, California. After their meal, Charles was playing one of those coin-operated games where you try to pick up a stuffed toy with a mechanical claw and drop it out the little chute. As he was working this machine, a stranger who was shabbily dressed but not really dirty approached him. The stranger asked Charles if he could have a ride toward Las Vegas. Charles agreed to give him a ride but told the stranger that he had to continue on to Los Angeles first, offload his current cargo, and reload with new cargo for a trip back East.

The stranger walked in front of Charles and Turkey Tracks as they left the truck stop and walked out across the huge parking lot toward their trucks. Charles said the man walked across the lot directly to his truck and got up in the right-hand passenger seat. This was odd because Charles hadn't mentioned which truck was his or which company he worked for, and the stranger hadn't asked. He just walked straight up to the right truck.

Charles and the stranger proceeded on to Los Angeles, where they offloaded and reloaded for the trip back East. Turkey Tracks had to unload his shipment at a different location, so the two drivers separated, each going his own way. After receiving a new load for the Eastern states, Charles and this mysterious rider ventured North on Interstate 15 toward Interstate 40. The rider was carrying a road atlas book with a leather cover that snapped shut when the maps were all folded up. The stranger started unfolding different maps and used them to show Charles what roads he would need to take to get back East. Then he started showing Charles maps of where he wanted to go in the Las Vegas area.

Much to Charles amazement, the stranger started telling him that he knew of the turmoil and serious problems that Charles was having in his life. He said he knew that things were so bad that Charles had been contemplating suicide. The stranger continued talking to Charles about several previous and very personal incidents that had led up to this turmoil—things that no one could possibly have known but Charles himself. It really seemed like the guy was reading his mind or something. But then the stranger said that God has a way of wrapping his arms around you when you're having troubles. He said that you just simply need to turn your problems over to God and let him wrap his arms around you and care for you. Needless to say, Charles found it very strange to hear all of this coming from the mouth of a complete stranger.

They continued on down the highway to Needles, California. They stopped at a restaurant and Charles offered to buy the stranger some coffee and a sandwich. The rider said no; he didn't really want anything. Charles suggested that he crawl up in the sleeper and rest a little bit, because he knew he had to be tired. The guy said okay; he'd do that. But after Charles ate and came back to the truck, the stranger had disappeared. The leather-bound atlas was still lying on the passenger seat, though. Charles opened it, revealing another mystery. Instead of the maps that the stranger had shown Charles earlier, each page in it was just a piece of white paper, blank except for the words "God loves you" printed on each one.

Much to his surprise, Charles heard Turkey Tracks on the CB as he approached Grants, New Mexico. The two of them stopped and had coffee together. Charles said that his rider sure had been a strange fellow. "What rider?" Turkey Tracks asked. Charles replied, "Well, the guy that I picked up in Ontario—the one that you and I walked out of the restaurant with." Turkey Tracks replied, "What rider? I didn't see any rider." Charles said, "You must have seen him. He walked in front of us all the way across the parking lot out to the trucks and then got up in the passenger seat of my truck." And Turkey Tracks said, "What are you talking about, man? What's wrong with you? Are you dreaming? There wasn't anybody walking in front of us. I never saw anybody get up in your truck."

After reaching Oklahoma City, Charles stopped at his sister's house for a short visit. His sister was a minister and Charles told her his strange story.

She said this rider must have been an angel sent by God to help Charles get through the tough times he was having in his life. She also asked to see the book of maps that had been transformed into white pages bearing the words "God loves you." Charles went out to the truck and retrieved the book. When he opened it, it contained the original maps he had seen when the stranger first opened up the book.

Very soon after this hard-to-comprehend experience, everything in Charles' life started becoming easier and more enjoyable again. He said that things just started coming together and that he was able to see the light at the end of the tunnel, so to speak. He was able to get his life straightened out and go on. Today, he believes that this angel probably saved his life, and he gives God credit for being all-powerful and all-loving.

CHAPTER TWENTY-FIVE

Face-to-Face with Jesus

Not long after Charles saw me in Sacramento, I had one of the most important soul travel experiences of my life. As it began, I found myself entering a large room through its back door. This room was long and rather narrow. The floor ran uphill toward the rear and was filled with seats. Looking around, I thought it must be a movie theater, but there was no screen, just a wall in the front with a small door on each side.

It was very light in this room and every seat was filled. There were also people standing along both walls and across the back of the room. I crowded against the back wall, taking what was nearly the last place left to stand. I soon realized that this huge crowd was saying something, and after listening to the guy standing next to me, I figured out everyone was chanting, "Jesus, I love you. Jesus, I love you." I don't know why, but I soon joined in the chant. I remember thinking that I surely must know somebody out of this many people, but about all I could see were the backs of their heads. There were both men and women, but no children.

As I stood there chanting along with everyone else, the door on the right side of the front wall opened and Jesus walked in. The crowd became quiet and I thought that surely Jesus was going to talk to us. There was a profound gentleness to him that is beyond my ability to communicate in words. He didn't look much like most of the pictures I'd seen of him over the years. He appeared to be about thirty years old with an olive-colored complexion and sandy, light-brown hair that fell to his shoulders but no further. He had very little facial hair—maybe two days' growth of beard, which was also pretty light in color. He was wearing a wheat-colored robe with a belt, or at least something tied around the middle of the robe.

Jesus looked straight ahead and walked slowly, never changing his facial expression. He then turned and walked toward the middle of the room and I could only see his left profile. As he approached a podium in the center of the room, I expected him to step up on a riser or maybe just turn toward the crowd; instead, I lost sight of him for a moment. I wasn't at all clear who or what had broken my line of sight with Jesus, but I jostled around for a better position without luck for a few seconds, to the point that I felt like I was being a bit rude to the people standing next to me. Of course, I didn't want to miss anything that Jesus might say or do.

Suddenly, I was able to see Jesus again, and by this point, he had passed the center of the room and was still walking slowly toward the back. I remember thinking that he was going to leave without saying anything. Almost at that same moment, he turned and continued toward the small door on the left side of the room. He opened the door, walked through it, and closed it behind him. I was very disappointed that he did not deliver some sort of message to us, although I was elated to have seen him.

As time has passed and I have thought much about the experience, I feel that Jesus delivered a message to at least some of the people in that room, but I was not allowed to hear it. Maybe I was not ready to accept his message for some reason, or maybe I did hear it and will remember it when the time is right.

CHAPTER TWENTY-SIX

The Death of Two Good Friends

As time went on, I learned that one of my friends named Joe, a man in his fifties, had been diagnosed with cancer in his kidneys. One kidney had been removed and the other stopped working, making it necessary for him to be on a dialysis machine three times a week. His doctors told him there was no hope for recovery and that he probably had less than a year to live.

I decided I would share some of my experiences with Joe. I planned to focus on the things I had been shown in my soul travels, especially the idea that our souls never die but simply use new bodies to help them learn and experience different situations in further lifetimes. At first, Joe had a little trouble believing my stories about the many soul travels I had experienced. After several visits, he became more comfortable and began asking a lot of questions. This made me feel good. In past years, I had wanted to try to help acquaintances that were terminally ill, but I never seemed to have the courage to approach such a touchy subject with any of them.

Joe became much more comfortable with the idea that when his present body gave up, he could look forward to another chance to fulfill the learning experience. He told me the hardest part of this new thinking was the fact that he knew me well enough to know I was telling him the truth. He would say, "If I didn't know you so well, I would think you were making up parts of these stories just to make me feel better."

During one of our visits, I mentioned that my dad had arthritis so bad that his fingers were twisted and swollen until the pain was nearly unbearable. Joe said that he knew a Native American man named Jack who could cure arthritis. Joe explained that Jack's father had been making a potion with this healing effect since the twenties, and he had passed the secret of its creation on to Jack.

Joe had asked Jack what he might be able to do for his cancer, but Jack told him that it was too far advanced to do much. However, Jack's potion cured Joe's gout, which had been very painful for quite some time. I introduced my dad to Jack, and two years after he started taking this liquid potion, he was free of his crippling arthritis. I truly was thankful for this knowledge gained from my dying friend.

After I shared the experiences I had while meditating with Willie, Joe said that he would really like to meet Willie and visit with him. I had lost contact with Willie over the past several years, but after several phone calls, I learned of his mother's phone number. I called and Willie answered the phone. I explained my friend's condition and his wish to meet for a short visit. Much to my surprise and disbelief, Willie said that we could drive down for a visit. But Willie added that we'd need to make this trip very soon because he himself had terminal stomach cancer and would be crossing over to the other side very soon. Willie was a young man in his thirties and this news devastated me.

We made the trip, which was hard for Joe to do because the two-hour ride caused him considerable pain. When we arrived at Willie's door, he told us to come on in. He was too weak to get up from his chair. My heart broke to see Willie in this condition, but we all three shared experiences and had a meaningful visit about life now, life in the past, and life in future incarnations. Willie had also described several personal contacts he had had with members of his family who had crossed over some years previously.

Soon Willie said he was completely out of strength and needed to take a nap, but then he arose from his chair, walked over to a bookshelf, and picked up the glass-like rock that he had let me hold during many of our meditation sessions several years earlier. He handed the rock to me and said that it had always loved me, so he wanted me to have it.

Fighting back the tears, we parted and started the trip back to Joe's home. He said he was very glad for the visit and that Willie had fortified my stories about the tunnel we pass through in order to reach the spiritual plane. Joe also said it was comforting to know that we never die; rather, we cast off an old body and move on.

About two weeks had passed after our visit with Willie when I learned that he had left this physical plane and crossed over. Joe hung on for another four or five months. I have always thought that if I hadn't taken time to visit Joe and help him prepare for the next step of crossing over, I would not have learned of Jack, who cured my dad's arthritis. I thought this was a wonderful trade because two people were helped.

CHAPTER TWENTY-SEVEN

More Psychic Experiences in the Physical

Like most people, I always dreamed about how neat it would be to strike it rich, win the lottery, or find a pot of gold at the end of a rainbow. As hard as I tried, I could never receive any type of message of an easy way to acquire riches. However, I did have one psychic experience that helped me to accumulate a little bit of money.

The experience happened in Las Vegas, Nevada, while I was playing blackjack. This was my fourth trip to the casinos in the past thirty years, but it was Jeannie's first time to visit. I was not a gambler or card player, and I always left Las Vegas with less money than I had arrived. On this trip, I slowly lost most of the money I had allocated for gambling at a blackjack table. Suddenly a strong feeling came over me. A force seemed to turn my head until I was looking at a group of slot machines. I knew one of them was going to pay me some money. I didn't know how much money, but I knew it would be good.

I folded my blackjack hand, slid down off the stool, and walked over to these machines. The feeling was strong as I walked down the aisle between the slot machines, but I realized I had no idea which of the fifty or more machines to try. I walked among them, becoming more and more frustrated. There were already people playing more than half of the machines, and I knew I did not have enough money to try them all.

I went to the other side of the room to find Jeannie. I told her about this unusual feeling and asked if she would try to get a feeling of which one of the machines I needed to put money into. She walked by all of them and then rounding a corner, she put her hand on a vacant machine and said, "This one." I put eight dollars in and hit a thousand dollar jackpot. After sharing half the money with her, I was thankful to be able to end that trip with more money than I'd started with.

It was around this same time that my son told me of a female psychic in Florida who had the ability to give a reading over the telephone if she had a recent picture of her subject's face. He explained that she had done this for him and her reading had been very on track with his life situation. He had come away from this experience feeling that she was a truly talented psychic.

I made a telephone appointment with this woman. The first thing she said to me was, "I see a very strong mother figure around you, serving as a guide and a guardian." I replied that my mother was still living. The psychic said that it must be a grandmother then, because the mothering instinct is very strong. I told her I felt it was my dad's mother because we had lived with my dad's parents on and off until I was nine years old, and I had always felt close to this grandmother.

The psychic added that she also saw a dog spirit very close to me, specifically a golden retriever. She found this very odd and asked if I had ever experienced closeness with a golden retriever. My reply was, "Yes, I'm experiencing it right now." My female golden retriever was lying at my feet as we spoke. I told her about my beloved old boxer and how she had appeared to me and given me a message. I also explained that I felt my golden retriever was the same spirit that had come back to be with me again. The lady said that yes, she was sure of this was a fact. The rest of the reading she did for me was very accurate, and much of what she foresaw came to pass in the several years following her reading. One of her predictions was that we would sell our home and move almost a thousand miles to live in another state.

Also in the early nineties, I became acquainted with a very spiritual psychic in Oklahoma City. His name is Wayne, and he has helped mold my philosophies. He has done several readings for me and other members of my family. His advice on directions to take and obstacles to avoid has helped many people get through difficult periods in their lives. He is a very gentle and kind man, and I feel he is truly a messenger for all the goodness in the universe. More than four months before the bombing of the Oklahoma City Murrah Federal Building in April of 1995, Wayne

A friend of mine took this image that shows hundreds of lightbeings of varying sizes.

went on public radio and warned of an upcoming disaster having to do with a protest against government. He had seen fire, smoke, and military personnel in the streets.

It seems as though my being is a magnet for spirits and spiritual energy on many levels. In fairly recent years, a friend and I were sitting in the living room of my home watching television. A huge ball that appeared to be made of light came flying through the room and seemed to land right beside my chair. Its energy was strong enough that it could easily be seen with the naked eye, and it actually lifted the leaves of a nearby plant as it moved under them. My friend saw it as well, and we both stared at each other in shock and amazement.

Several years after this incident, LeeAnn Sharpe, the woman who edited the first version of my life story, took a few photos of me with her digital camera. Every image of me she captured showed orbs attached to my body but not to anyone else's. Even when she used different angles to photograph me, she still found these orbs in every one.

I don't fully understand what orbs are, and I'm not sure that anyone else does, either. They appear most of the time as small balls of light. For the most part, researchers believe that they consist of electromagnetic energy. I have read that a theoretical physicist who has worked for over a decade at the Los Alamos National Laboratory in New Mexico has determined that orbs are energy and heat. Most of the time, they cannot be seen by the naked eye, but this is not always the case—I have personally seen several of them.

Much of the time, these orbs will show up on film. I have taken pictures of them with a simple old 35mm camera and I have seen many pictures of orbs taken with newer digital cameras. I have a picture taken by a friend of mine that shows over fifty orbs surrounding her motor home. They are all different sizes; the smallest are roughly the size of silver dollars while the largest are five or six times larger than basketballs.

In discussing orb sightings with several people, I have learned that some people can see them most of the time with the naked eye while other people cannot see them at all. I realize that radio and TV waves travel through the air with some type of energy and cannot be seen. This makes it easier for me to understand that orbs might do the same thing. I don't know if having orbs around you that show up on film is a good thing, a bad thing, or neither.

I have visited with a couple of crop circle investigators who have spent a lot of time performing studies in the U.S. and especially in England. They both say that orbs are often seen around newly formed crop circles. It is a mystery whether orbs are a natural part of Earth's energy or whether they perhaps have a spiritual nature controlled by someone or something in a different dimension.

CHAPTER TWENTY-EIGHT

A Big Move and More Out-of-Body Family Reunions

By the late eighties, Jeannie and I were pretty much ready to leave Oklahoma for good. I'd lived in the state my entire adult life, and I was finally getting fed up with the constant high winds and the tornadoes we got every spring. I was also tired of living on the same property for so long—Jeannie, Julie, and I had lived in the same home in Banner for the past thirteen years, mainly because we didn't want to pull Julie out of her school and away from her friends. And I was especially sick of the small workshop on my fifteen-acre property from which I ran my used truck business.

After Julie graduated from high school, Jeannie and I began seriously considering other areas of the country to live in. The first possibility we explored was Florida. But after a trip there, we discovered that we weren't thrilled with either the climate or the culture of the area. It took us a few years and a few more trips before we finally settled on the Phoenix area as the ideal location for our new home. We moved to New River, just outside of Phoenix, on the very last day of 1994. I continued essentially the same business I'd been doing in Oklahoma—buying and selling used trucks and trailers of various types.

Following this big move, I've only experienced one substantial soul travel. In it, I found myself in a group of several people. I turned to see who was standing near me and saw a line of women standing near a counter. My dad's mother stood at the very back of this line. She had crossed over some twenty years ago. I had forgotten how short she was—less than five feet tall. She didn't say anything to me, but she had a really big smile. She also looked to be fifty years old, not the eighty-five that she had lived to be on this earthly plane.

My father had crossed over in June 1994, and although I have not seen him in any of my soul travels, my sister's grown son Josh has seen his spirit three times. He spoke only once, saying, "Josh, where is Gene?"

My mother had always enjoyed listening to the stories of my out-of-body experiences. My father, on the other hand, would get up and leave the room whenever I began to speak about them. When I was not around, he would scold my mother harshly for listening to my stories and taking them seriously. He felt that this was only encouraging what he saw as my foolishness. "There's got to be something wrong with Gene that he believes all of this stuff," my father would tell my mother, "And there's got to be something wrong with you for listening to him."

My mother never told me about the scoldings my father gave her when I wasn't around, but she did tell Jeannie, who conveyed the information to me. Jeannie told me I needed to stop talking about my soul travels with my mother so that I wouldn't get her into further trouble with my father. Now that my father has crossed over, I'd sure like to know how his opinions about all my "crazy stories" may have changed.

Before my dad died, I had left a small gasoline engine and some other parts at his shop for him to repair for me. Years before that, back in the sixties, he had sold small riding lawnmower tractors. The brand name he sold was Wheel Horse. He had kept one of these old ones for over forty years. I had always thought that my dad, my brother, or I would recondition this old mower tractor and have it in the family as a keepsake. It had been sitting outside in the same spot for several years, and I don't remember any of us telling mother about our plans to revamp it and keep it in the family.

Shortly after my father's passing, some people my mother had known since she was a teenager came by the old shop. Spotting this old Wheel Horse tractor, they realized it had some value as a collectible and asked her if they could have it. She said, "Sure, you can have it." As they were loading it in their truck, they noticed my engine and some other parts sitting there. My mother ended up giving all of this stuff to them. The next time I visited my mother and discovered everything she had given away, I became very upset. I scolded her for not calling me or my brother and asking for our opinions. Thinking back later, I must've been overly critical and very harsh with her.

Soon after this event, my mother was in bed, close to being asleep, with her old dog sleeping on the floor next to her. The dog began to growl. She said this was something he had never done before. She said that the hair on the back of the dog's neck was standing straight up and he continued to growl. Then a very strange feeling came over my mother, and she soon realized that her own father was standing at the foot of her bed. She was elated to see him, of course. He said not to worry about the things that she had given away because the family she had given them to were good people who meant well. He also said that this family had actually done some things to help her when she was younger.

My mother said that Jesus appeared at that point, standing behind her father with his eyes glowing brightly. She related that even though this very odd occurrence frightened her, she was overjoyed to see her dad in the company of Jesus. In the days that followed, she seemed to be happier and not so torn about my scolding. I then started to beat myself up pretty badly over what I had said to my mother, and I continued to do so for several years. I realized how insignificant some old pieces of iron were and how crazy it was for me to cause my mother pain. As far as I know, this was the only type of spiritual experience that she ever had.

Obviously, some of the most memorable psychic experiences that I or other members of my family have involved seeing some of our family members who had passed on in previous years. Other than my own relatives, the only other person that I ever even recognized in any of my travels was Jesus. But when I think back on my soul travels in general, one thing that is strange to me was how I felt the same loving attraction for all of the spirits, both male and female, that I encountered. It was never important whether it was a male or female spirit. On Earth, you have sexual feelings between a man and woman. But between spirits on the heavenly plane, those feelings don't exist. I found myself just happy to be in the company of a soul brother or sister, but there was never any sexual attraction at all.

I always had the feeling that every spirit I came across was busy working on its own soul development. As I've mentioned before, they never really stopped to hang out; they were always busy doing something. My guess is that they have a sense that lets them know what they need to be doing to further the development of their souls.

Another somewhat strange aspect of these spirits was that almost every single one I ever saw appeared to be adults of about fifty years of age. I never once saw any children. Even when I saw my grandfather and grandmother in separate soul travels, both looked to be about fifty, even though they had each lived to the age of eighty-five. One of the only two exceptions was Jesus, who looked about thirty. The other exception occurred when I was brought in front of the twelve reverent men I discussed earlier. These men all looked very old and wise—maybe eighty or ninety years old.

CHAPTER TWENTY-NINE

Working for Hospice

Two years after we'd moved to Phoenix, I wound up volunteering my services to VistaCare Hospice, an organization dedicated to easing the final months of life for people who have been determined by doctors to have less than six months left to live. I explained to the folks who ran this group that I felt like I had been blessed with the many psychic experiences I had been given over the course of my life, and I was now looking to find a way to give back a little to others.

After I'd described some of my out-of-body experiences to Mike, one of the group's organizers, he told me that he thought that some of the patients that the group dealt with would like to hear my stories. "Since these people are at the end of their lives, many of them are worried about going to hell. Or they're wondering if heaven actually exists," Mike explained. "Since you've had all of these firsthand spiritual experiences, I think it might make some of these people feel better to hear you describe them." I was very surprised to hear him say this but quite pleased. I had expected to be mowing lawns or buying groceries for people who could no longer do such things for themselves, but this sounded much more interesting.

Mike went with me on my first visit to a hospice patient. He sat and listened as I told the patient about some of the many ways in which I had been shown that life goes on after the death of the physical body. The patient seemed grateful to hear about these experiences, and Mike was thrilled with the results my stories had in lightening the patient's anxieties about dying. After that, he sent me by myself to meet quite a few different hospice patients.

There was a patient named Fred I visited a good number of times who was exceptionally curious to know what happened after death. Of all the hospice patients I talked with, he certainly had the greatest interest in the stories of my out-of-body travels. Each time I would come and tell him about some of my soul travel experiences, he'd get so engrossed in them and ask me so many questions that I'd end up staying and talking with him for several hours.

The last time I visited Fred, he was very, very near the end of his life. The veil gets very thin when you're about to cross over, and Fred had gotten to the point where he could see his grandmother who had crossed over herself quite a few years earlier. It made Fred very happy to see with his own eyes that there was in fact life after death and know that his grandmother was happily awaiting their reunion on the other side.

One day when I was at the hospice office, I overheard a conversation among the organizers about how they needed a woman for some advertising that they were planning. My mind immediately went to Jeannie, whom I've always thought was an exceptionally beautiful woman. Now you might well accuse me of being biased on this score, but I certainly wasn't the only one to admire her looks. With the encouragement of her beautician, Jeannie had begun entering beauty pageants specifically for married women in the last few years we lived in Oklahoma. Despite the fact that Jeannie was in her late forties and competing against women almost thirty years younger, she had been crowned Mrs. Oklahoma in 1993 and Mrs. Arizona in 1996.

I mentioned to the hospice organizers that I was married to the current Mrs. Arizona, and their ears perked up. They were clearly quite interested in using her as a spokesperson. Their only reservations stemmed, I suppose, from thoughts of a stereotypical bubbleheaded beauty queen. "Can she walk and chew gum at the same time?" was one of the questions they asked me. I assured them that Jeannie was college educated and plenty intelligent, as well as being a good speaker.

So VistaCare put Jeannie to work, initially in a volunteer capacity. After a short while, they were so impressed with her that they hired her as a full-time employee at a good salary. Jeannie loved the job and threw herself into it wholeheartedly.

CHAPTER THIRTY

Losing My Soul Mate and Best Friend

Jeannie's job with VistaCare involved a lot of speaking engagements. In the summer of 1998, after she'd been working for the organization for about two years, she began noticing a little bit of a cough or a catch in her throat during the speeches she gave. We were concerned about this, so we asked the doctors at VistaCare to take a look at Jeannie's throat. They didn't seem to think there was a serious problem.

So Jeannie continued her speaking engagements, but the cough slowly got worse over time and really began to bother her. We consulted another doctor who told us that he believed Jeannie had a case of something called Valley Fever. We'd never heard of this, but the doctor explained that it was caused by certain fungi entering the lungs, carried there by wind or dust. He prescribed some antibiotics and said they should take care of the problem.

Rather than getting better over time with the medication, Jeannie's cough just continued to get worse. We consulted another doctor who took x-ray of Jeannie's chest. He found that there was some type of abnormality in Jeannie's left lung about the size of a hen's egg that was pushing on her windpipe. The doctor took some cultures from Jeannie and ran tests on them, finally concluding, like the previous doctor, that this was a case of Valley Fever. He also prescribed a similar course of treatment as the last doctor. Again, this didn't seem to help at all. If anything, Jeannie's cough just grew worse.

We went to yet another doctor who told us that, unfortunately, the abnormality in Jeannie's lung that the previous x-rays had uncovered could be a cancerous growth. The doctor went in through Jeannie's back and ribs to take a culture of the abnormality. The tests he ran on this culture showed it to be very cancerous.

A young surgeon advised Jeannie that the best course of action would be to remove her left lung. He assured her that she should be fine afterward and that people had been known to live as long as thirty-five years with just one lung. The surgeon strongly convinced Jeannie that this was the right course, but he didn't convince me. I was against the idea and fought Jeannie on this decision for some time, but she finally talked me into it.

The surgeon removed Jeannie's lung in November of 1998. The surgery was hard on her, but by January of the following year, she had returned to her job at hospice, working half-time. In March she started getting some tremendous headaches; they wouldn't last very long, but they were intensely painful when they happened.

One Sunday afternoon while I was at the car races, Jeannie was at home when an especially painful headache hit her. The pain was so strong that she couldn't drive, so she had some neighbors take her to the hospital. A young intern at the hospital insisted that they do some type of scan of Jeannie's brain to see what was wrong. He found cancerous lesions all over her brain.

I was crushed. I took Jeannie to every cancer doctor I'd ever heard of, and we just did everything we could possibly do to fight the cancer. We even made weekly visits to several clinics down in Mexico that assured us they could cure Jeannie. Nothing worked and Jeannie just kept getting worse and worse. Finally, she crossed over on November 8, 1999, which devastated my life.

CHAPTER THIRTY-ONE

The Past Decade

Jeannie had been my best friend for over twenty years. After she crossed over, I grew considerably closer to my son Chris. Chris was living near Phoenix at that point, and I hired him to work part time for me in my business. He and I invested in stocks together too, and Chris would use the computer in my office to complete our stock sales and purchases. We also ate at least one meal together every day. In this period, Chris became my new best friend.

Chris crossed over tragically on February 16, 2003, and that devastated my life again. I don't want to go into details about his death, but suffice it to say that he lost his life over a worthless woman.

My daughter Raquel now lives in Alabama. Her husband retired from the Air Force as a Lieutenant Colonel at the age of 41 and is now working for a company that sends satellites into space. Raquel works as a hairdresser, and has two children. As of this writing, one is a senior in high school and the other is a senior in college.

My daughter Julie lives in Phoenix, where she runs a business called Long Term Care Solutions that helps older people with their business affairs. She is married and very much wants a child; she has been through great struggles in recent years attempting to adopt one.

As I have mentioned before, my soul travels began happening less and less as the years went on, and I have only had a handful in the past decade. One of the last times that I am aware of it happening, my soul only traveled about a foot above my body. I knew exactly where I was and what was happening. As my soul floated just above my prone body in the bed below, I remember thinking, "Okay, I hope I get to go somewhere else and see something new." Then I could feel my soul make another effort to move a little further from my body, but this was quickly followed by a feeling of extreme exhaustion. I could tell that I was just too tired to make anything more of this sad little attempt at soul travel; I just didn't have the energy.

Recently, in the summer of 2011, I have started to see glimpses of what seems to be a human figure in my home. These glimmers are quite reminiscent of the angels that I described seeing in an earlier chapter—an experience that always happened outdoors and usually in the presence of horses. I still live in the same home in Phoenix that Jeannie and I shared for the last several years of her life, which is also the place that she crossed over. So I can't help but wonder if this form I'm getting brief glimpses of is Jeannie's soul. If it is, I wish she could give me some kind of a sign to let me know it's her.

CHAPTER THIRTY-TWO

Conclusion

After many years of thinking about my many soul-travel experiences, I have tried to analyze the lessons I have been given through them. For years, whenever I thought about God, the universe, how things really work, and the love we all need to learn here on Earth, I always felt like I had so much to learn. But I now believe that I honestly don't have anything to learn at all. I believe that I have learned it all many, many times in the past and that I already know it somewhere deep inside—I just have a tremendous amount to remember. My hangups and the pain within me from the way I've acted and not shown love to every other soul on Earth have blocked these memories. But I sincerely hope I will be able to remember everything I have learned in my past lives by meditating and filling my heart with a love that I can share with everyone on planet Earth.

I think a soul chooses to reincarnate into a situation that allows it to do good for others that it might have been wronged in the past, and also to repay those who have exerted much effort to be helpful to it in previous incarnations. I believe most souls reincarnate into a circle of family and friends who are trying to help each other through the generations to reach our ultimate goal of embracing the gifts of heaven. It seems that some souls might even find the right life situation to further their learning experience and reincarnate into a new body very soon after crossing over.

I also have reason to believe many souls wait as long as what would be several hundred years in our measurement of time before feeling the need or finding the right life situation to reincarnate into this Earth plane. I realize that for many people who have spent their lifetimes learning the conventional religious doctrines taught in our modern-day churches, the idea of the soul using many different bodies through various lifetimes in its quest to get back to our heavenly home is hard to believe.

I also think when a very young baby dies and no medical reason can be found, its soul has decided for some reason not to remain and live out that particular lifetime. Maybe after more consideration, the soul sees the lessons that lie ahead are not important at that time. Or perhaps the soul sees a more important opportunity coming in the near future and simply leaves its new body, never to return to it.

I feel that we should not be totally controlled by the doctrines taught by organized religion. We must make peace within ourselves and learn to be spiritual in nature with our Creator. Also, we must learn to live in harmony with our fellow man and offer help gladly and constantly to make everyone else's lives easier and their spiritual journeys more pleasant. When it is your turn to stand in front of the light, your preacher won't be there telling you what to do or what is going to happen next. If your preacher hasn't experienced standing at the far end of the tunnel and being embraced by the all-loving white light, he or she doesn't really know any more about what is going to happen than you do. I can assure you that memorizing a few Bible verses and going to school to hone your speaking skills won't gain you passage into the light or an invitation to stay on the heavenly plane.

The review of your deeds while you were on this earthly plane will be a personal one. When you cross over for the last time and stay there, you will be your own judge. There won't be a panel of judges reading out a list of the sins you committed during your time on Earth—you will judge yourself. You're the one who knows exactly what you've done to help others or hurt others and you will be far harder on yourself than any panel of judges could ever be. I haven't judged myself in any of my trips to the other side, but I have come close.

It is only at this point of self-judgment that you will fully feel the pain you caused others and enjoy the goodness you have extended. This could be as simple as regretting you did not stop to help someone with a flat tire because your lifestyle was so rushed that you had to be somewhere at a certain time to help yourself to something better. During the review of your deeds, you may possibly see that this fellow brother or sister may have had a sick child in the vehicle that needed medical attention badly, and possibly your stopping to help could've been very important to them.

I've been to heaven many times in my soul travels, and it is very different than the way people on Earth tend to envision it. There are no pearly gates. But I do know that we are all going to heaven when we cross over for good. There is no devil, there is no hell, and there is no purgatory. We're all going to the same place, but we're not all going to be that happy with ourselves when we get there. Someone like Mother Theresa is probably going to be flitting around heaven having a good time after she completes her own self-judgment. But some of us are going to be pretty disappointed in our behavior and pretty hard on ourselves during and after self-judgment. That's your real punishment right there—that's your hell.

I know that God loves all souls and we are all one. Skin color, race, origin of birth, and religious beliefs have nothing to with the entire human race being brothers and sisters. When we do anything that hurts another, we are simply hurting ourselves. The very opposite is also true: When we actually do something good and make an effort to help someone else, we are helping all humankind as well as ourselves. I don't know who coined the golden rule, but it is one of the most famous phrases floating around our planet. I often wonder if this would possibly be all we would need to know and practice for a successful life here on Earth. "Do unto others as we would have them do unto us" might be the secret for a successful, happy life here on Earth. It honestly might be the only thing we would need to know to further our soul development and end up at our heavenly home.

I was delighted to learn that animals have souls and that our pets come back again and again to be with us. My golden retriever was the reincarnation of our boxer named Honey. My wife's black Labrador was the same soul as the female Scotty that she had when we first met. The lab had so many of the same traits and behaviors as the old Scotty did that it was almost impossible to believe they were not the same soul in different bodies.

I am comfortable with the thought that Jeannie is my soul mate and that our many past lives together caused the love at first sight we both experienced nearly twenty years ago. As I explained earlier, she and I were both married to other people when we met. The attraction we had to each other must have been rooted deeply in all the many lifetimes we have shared in the past, helping one another in trying to progress toward our spiritual home. Even though I don't know the exact reasons we didn't meet and marry at a younger age, I can accept the fact that we both had other obligations to fulfill and separate learning experiences we needed to encounter alone early in this lifetime. While we were together, we enjoyed talking about the many things we have learned from each other and also the areas in which we can improve ourselves to help shorten our paths homeward.

The following quote describes Jeannie's feelings about our time together. She said, "From the first time we met, it seemed as though we had prior knowledge of how the other felt about a lot of things. There were no uncomfortable pauses as there usually are when two people begin to try to get to know one another. We both love animals and the outdoors. Family and children are very important to us. We like living in the country and neither of us seems to fit into the corporate world. We both believe that spirituality is more important than what religion you belong to. We both know that we have been on this Earth plane together in earlier times and that we will reincarnate into lives that will bring us together again. We both believe that each incarnation brings us closer to what is commonly called heaven. We both have respect and love for the Earth and nature. For me, the only explanation is that we already knew each other when we met in this lifetime and that we are meant to be together."

It is also my belief that our Earth is constantly visited by superior life forms. I think they try to guide us and help us in many different ways. It is very possible they are acting as teachers, trying to get us to care for Mother Earth and not abuse her resources, which can easily give us everything we need to sustain life. After all, when we are born back into a future generation, we will have to live with whatever conditions we have left our planet in.

These superior life forms probably have the ability to walk among us and promote love and respect for all living creatures. Most people cannot accept the idea of beings of superior intelligence walking among us; a lot of chaos would certainly occur if they were open about their existence. I hope our future generations will learn to welcome them as missionaries and accept their offers of guidance, much as our own underdeveloped nations are gradually accepting this generation's teaching of a better lifestyle through self-improvement. I am thankful we live in a society where we have freedom of choice to do what best fulfills our personal needs.

It is my belief that congregating with friends and neighbors in a conventional church house for a service is fine for anyone who feels the need. I have personally had a number of experiences in nature that caused me to feel closer to my Creator than anything I have experienced in a formal church service. A crisp mountain morning at sunrise, a clear mountain lake, or a beautiful tree silhouetted against a magnificent sunset will always put me in awe of Mother Nature.

I know life is precious and the body we have to use during each lifetime is a divine gift. There are indications that there aren't enough bodies available for every soul awaiting another chance to learn. We need to treat our bodies as temples—after all, they are home to our very beings. The body is a marvelous creation, more so than any machine that man has made, but it requires some care. Any type of overindulgence—whether it be food, drink, or work—can shorten the brief time we have to learn the necessary lessons that we came into this physical realm to learn in the first place.

Probably the worst thing we could do is to shorten the chance of fellow souls to live out their chosen reincarnations, and very possibly the second worst act would be to alter our own time on this plane. However, one of the greatest deeds performed might be the miracle of giving birth and nurturing a new life. I think our Creator has a special love and admiration for mothers who perform this feat to the best of their abilities, whether they be animal or human.

I believe we can carry out many small acts of goodness that will help us on our journeys, such as showing patience and compassion for senior citizens. There might be a time when they walk or drive too slowly to suit our fast pace of life, but if some of them had not pioneered this land and helped to build a free country, we might not have anywhere to go in such a hurry.

I have no clue as to why I was chosen to experience travels beyond the physical for forty or so years. I came into this life a humble farm boy and my education and lifestyle have been very ordinary and basic. For the first thirty years of these unexplained happenings, I was too scared and embarrassed to discuss them with strangers. Now I am seventy, and after considering how much work and effort several beings from the other side have exerted to show me the many adventures our souls can look forward to, I needed to tell my story. I am happy I can share with you the knowledge that to leave the present body behind and cross over will be another step in our glorious trip toward life everlasting.

I know that the many places that I have visited, the different planes and planets that I have been shown, and the place we call heaven are not somewhere far beyond the clouds. These places are actually quite close to us; they simply exist in different dimensions from the physical one in which we reside.

My prayer for my fellow man is that each day you awaken, you will give thanks to all the goodness in the universe for another chance to go forward with faith and for being allowed this time in eternity. I pray each of us will work hard to enhance the journeys of others so that the day will come when we all can remain in that joyous place, our heavenly home.

Part Two

Out-Of-Body Experiences

Channeled Commentary and Explanations through Robert Shapiro

CHAPTER THIRTY-THREE

Angelic Being

Interpreted by Zoosh through Robert Shapiro

22 AUGUST 2011

[Unintelligable and very soft sounds.]

Zoosh will be acting as interpreter. Now, the being coming through is unable to adapt to your current Earth language. It is from the future when you have a single language on Earth—but not a language that exists now, except in very ancient times. So I am speaking as the personality of that being, who is an instructor in the angelic world and interpreter of ancient languages, but who apparently has never come across this one, with the translation currently happening with the aid of Zoosh. So it might be slow going here for a little while.

The being of the future has an unpronounceable name in your language, though the sounds you heard at the beginning were its name, most likely impossible for you to spell—someday maybe. Question?

So this is a different angelic than the one I talked to last week.

It is always like that, but it is not a problem. Can answer your questions. Getting better now.

Okay. The subject is out-of-the-body experiences. On Earth now, that's what we call them, but I think that this really is the person being partly awake and aware when the soul goes out of the body at night on its nightly visits and then remembering some of these experiences on awakening. Isn't that correct?

That's really it. It's defined like that because the person involved recalls the experience, as you say, but of course everybody does this. So as you say, exactly: It is a recollection of that. So if a person recalls it, unless they are very young, it is intended for them to recall it. Most likely, the arrangement was made before the physical birth, once the baby had confirmed that it would stay—meaning the soul in the baby would have confirmed that it would stay in physical life for a time. So usually the arrangement is made, then, before birth.

But you are inquiring about an individual—I've looked at that a little bit already—and that individual did something different. He requested before life to have contacts with old friends, and when the inquiry was made by the angelics and guides, really in the moments before the moving out from mother, the soul in the baby requested that "all,"—just like this, not in this sequence, but all—"old friends encounter," something like that, see? That's the best interpretation. I don't know if you know this, but souls inside their mothers speak, continue to communicate, in the same language that is the universal language of many planets and also the language that exists in the future on Earth. So the direct interpretation I just gave you was as good as it gets in your language.

The reason that the encounters, then, took place in the way they did is that sometimes friends would be from other planets. They would look different when they were not here, but his soul wanted—however naively, yes, as souls are—to have these encounters because his soul was frightened of living on Earth but was doing that Earth life because he felt, on the basis of his teachers, that it would be good to do for the growth of his soul.

So if this person is still around or if you know him, you can tell him that his soul has grown sufficiently and he need not think about these matters anymore—unless he is still having the visitations. And if the visitations are troubling, all he has to do is say these words out loud just once. Just say: "I am asking to be able to live my Earth life now in the most benevolent and uncomplicated fashion." That's all. You just say it out loud. If for any reason you can't speak out loud, whispering is adequate. Try to say it at a time when there are no distractions so you can pay attention to the words. If for people, since this covers other people—I realize you're asking that for this specific person but also for others . . .

Yes, I want this for everyone.

Yes, I understand. If the people who are saying these words have interactions with spiritual energies and you feel the energy come up before the words are spoken, just wait, because this will be the beings getting ready to establish that for you. And then wait until the energy fades a bit, then start to stay the words. If the energy comes up again, also wait. Always do that when making such requests. And if by the time you're done saying those words the energy there is strong for a while, then just wait until it fades just about all the way. It may not fade completely for some of you, especially those of you who are sensitive to such energies; it might go on for hours.

But wait until it has faded almost completely, and then you can move about slowly. If the energy is that strong for some of you, then you might want to move very slowly if you need to for the next two hours. But if perhaps you've said this before sleep, then you can just go to sleep. If you are saying this at a time when you are sleeping with somebody else, I strongly recommend that you sleep in a different bed. Just tell them that you're going to say special prayers or whatever's appropriate in your family, and they'll probably be all right with that.

Okay. This particular man—his name is Gene Schmitz—is on the other end of the equation. He hasn't had these experiences for forty years, and he would definitely like them. Can he say something to have them start again?

Well, I'll have to say to him—and others who may have this situation—that if the experiences stop, it was probably because there was a conflict between living life on Earth, interacting with other peoples, loved ones, and so on, and having these experiences that his loved ones or the culture that he was in may not have been able to accept very well. So there would have been a confusion and a need to be physical on Earth.

I would recommend an alternative, all right? The decision has been made to stop the experiences, so what I would recommend is to ask to have these experiences in dreams, and ask for them to take place benevolently and enjoyably and to be able to remember those dreams. Should I give the exact words?

Yes, please.

I would recommend, then, that one say—like with the other thing—just say, "I am asking to be able to have the most benevolent dreams and visions that remind me of those wonderful experiences that I remember from my youth." Like that. So we're going to emphasize the word "remember," because one does not always remember everything, eh?

These experiences started for him at age thirteen, and for years he would hover up in the corner of the roof, looking down at his body. Now, that's because he was afraid. You said there was a fear of Earth life, right?

Yes, and there was also somewhat of a judgment of the physical form of the human being. This particular person—and many who have experiences like this—has not lived in a physical body on Earth. They have lived in human bodies before on other planets, but human bodies on other planets are a little different. So on Earth, there was a feeling of discomfiture with the physical form.

Okay. Now, all of those spirits that he saw for those years that would pass him by—were these spirits his old friends? I mean . . . not passing by, but he would see from his little perch there on the ceiling, coming and going.

All of the beings that he would see that would pass by, so to speak, or that he would pass by—they were all old friends, yes, every one. And more importantly, he's seen some of them at the deepest dream level since then, and he will see them all again, of course.

When he leaves the body, yes. Now, he hated for the night to come, because when he got out of the body, it would be so painful when he went slammed back in. He would just feel like he was beat up. That's not normal, is it?

It is, in fact, not so unusual, because when a soul is out of the body in that fashion, it is in its complete and natural state, as natural as it can be. If someone was in the room, he would feel like he was physical, like he was a person, all right? But if someone was in the room and was perceptive, he or she would just see a dot of light. But from his perspective, he would feel himself as a physical person, and he would feel lite, but not L-I-G-H-T: He would feel L-I-T-E, lightweight. So when he would go back into the physical body, he would feel heavy. He would feel like . . . imagine yourself suddenly picking up a backpack that weighed forty pounds and not being used to carrying such a thing. It would be like a heavy weight.

He also he had difficulty—and this is not rare—dealing with the digestive tract of the human body. Now, the big difference between Earth human physical bodies and the human physical bodies that one finds on other planets is very much involved with the digestive tract. The digestive tract, generally speaking, on other planets is much simpler—there are nowhere near the complications. The liver is more the size of a node, that small. The spleen and so on, such other organs, pancreas and all that, are barely noticeable, because the body does not have to sort of do battle to survive. On Earth, these organs are much more defined, and even the length of the intestine is vastly longer on Earth.

So the real difficulty was the digestive system. Now, this is not rare. For many souls who are experiencing an Earth human body of these times—in the past 10,000 years or so, maybe longer—the big struggle is dealing not so much with the heart and the lungs, even though they might be a little smaller on other planets, but the big struggle is dealing with the digestive system, and not even with the stomach, although in the stomach on other planets the digestive juices are not as volatile. So the big problem is basically the digestive system, and as a result, it creates a feeling of resistance to being a physical Earth human.

Sometimes what helps with that—but not for everyone—is if you are able to swim in a location where the water is very clear and pure. Now, that's not easy to find these days, and I'm not talking about swimming pools. If there are dolphins or sea turtles in the water, then the combination of energies from those two types of beings with this affinity and this contact with probably saline water in the sea can sometimes create a feeling of safety and comfort and ease on the planet. Or this just simply works with dolphins, who have an affinity with all life forms on Earth, and they're the only beings on Earth like that, period. The issue is, though, that the dolphins must be free. They cannot be captive. If they are captive, it doesn't work, because they will be frustrated and upset. So they have to be natural.

So it is possible, perhaps, to find places like that left on Earth. So it would not be guaranteed that it would be a cure, but 60 to 63 percent of people would feel vastly better being in a physical human Earth body after an experience like that of anywhere from ten minutes to forty minutes, okay? Now, for those who would not feel vastly better, they would feel somewhat better.

So that's something that he married her. He and his second wife felt that they were soul mates, that they had had many, many, many lives on Earth, that they were totally connected. So if he had never been on Earth before, had he been with this particular woman many times on other planets?

Yes, and that is the path for him, you see—and it's not unusual for people who make this type of request before birth. So, yes, and as hard as that was for the person he was married to previously, I can understand why he chose to do that.

Okay. Well, he went to psychics whose focus was on past Earth lives, and they gave him past Earth lives to explain that connection, but awareness of lives on other planets may not be part of their belief system. Also he feels that soul of the dog, a boxer, that he loved so much came back into his next dog, but we have talked about the immortal personalities of dogs through Robert for the **Animal Souls Speaks** ***book, and they say that they made a commitment for only one life on Earth. Did this particular soul actually come back into that next dog body—I think it was a retriever?***

I believe what occurred in that situation is that the dog personality made various fleeting appearances. This is not unknown: It's not that that soul is there . . .

Oh, it's like walking in and out, checking in and out while the original soul of the dog is still there.

Yes, fleeting appearances, enough so that the bond can be made. I feel that there was grief at the loss of that previous . . .

Yes, tremendous grief. He felt guilty.

Yes, but the soul did make fleeting appearances and that allowed the person to then have the feeling of familiarity and, most importantly, forgiveness.

Yes, and love. His second wife, Jeannie, the soul mate, loved horses and rode horses. Gene had been seeing what he thought were angels around the place for two or three weeks, and he said that he didn't see any wings, but these beings were about the same size as humans and moving in different directions five or six feet above the ground. Jeannie said she didn't see anything, but she had experienced a strange feeling of a presence when she was giving horse-riding lessons. And a couple of days after that, the old mare suddenly just stopped and stared, and his eyes were huge. And that's the only time he ever did anything like that. What were they all seeing? Were they angels, or what did the horse see?

Lightbeings. Very often, lightbeings—especially if they're giving off white or gold light—will literally be angels. Angels, you understand, do not actually have wings, but the fact that they are airborne . . . originally, they were painted that way in the past, and people spoke of them that way. And there are some beings who have wings, but they do not necessarily fly with those wings. You will not find people who will say that the wings moved the way a bird's wings do. You won't find that. So they were lightbeings. In the case of the horse, the horse did see a being he didn't expect to see, someone who was known to him, a being who had passed over.

The horse did not expect to see that, but because of the energy of the area, it was possible to see this. One often has these experiences when—speaking in this case about nonhumans—the humans aren't around. Just because one experiences these things around humans does not mean it was the only time it happened, okay? So with that particular being, it was not the only time. It just didn't expect to see that other being.

And the horse saw someone it knew personally who had died, that's what you said?

Yes.

Okay. He did see the boxer. He says, "This particular trip out of the body had the strangest magnetic pull sensation I'd ever encountered. It pulled me along, doing somersaults and twirling and finally moving me in a straight line." It took him to see his grandfather, and his grandfather had a message for his mother.

Sometimes there is this tumbling, twirling feeling. That is usually done to keep someone safe. If you're encountering another being you know, if there was tumbling and twirling—and in ET situations sometimes that's just done to amuse children—but in this particular situation, I believe it was done because it helped to insulate the being who was on his way to visit his grandfather. Sometimes you cannot take a straight line, because . . . you have to remember, he was still fairly young then, and it's easy to take on things when you are young—or even youthful. Sometimes people are young at heart, and they will take on things for others. Dogs do this all the time. All dogs are young at heart, even when they are very old. So that was the issue. He was being insulated, and the tumbling business was insulating.

Now, he would have guides that would go along with him, but then never talked to him, or they wouldn't answer his questions. He says, "I knew whatever and wherever I would be shown was important to someone in the spiritual realm or they would not have sent these guys. I never understood why they never talked to me or answered my questions or why they seemed so cold toward me. I never recognized any of them." Can you say something about these guides who would come and take him places but not tell him why or what it meant or talk to him or anything?

For one thing, you have to keep in mind that beings like that are not intended to communicate with worded language, all right? It is all done the way it was done, but it's not intended that they speak, and also it was not intended for him to form a kinship or a bond with those beings. They were simply—how can you say?—like "follow the leader"-type beings. So they were there so that he wouldn't get lost, but they were not there to be friends.

Okay. They took him once to a plane—he calls these different places where they took him planes—where he heard the most beautiful music he'd ever heard in his entire life, "like a thousand bells all playing at once, each playing a different sound and usually a different color . . . many voices singing softly." What were they, and why did they take him there?

That's as close as you can describe heaven, really. After life, one often experiences souls who are either coming in to be born or souls who are leaving. It's sort of a transitional place. People who have had after-death experiences and then come back have sometimes described this.

Yes, near-death experiences.

And this is a typical thing one finds for those who are blessed enough to have had the experience. So that was a gift.

Okay, now this next one is weird. He says, "Another travel ended in a strange but very real place. We wound up at a concrete building. I traveled to a huge room with a half-moon-shaped table that was large enough for twelve men to sit behind. This table was arranged so that all twelve could see each other and all could see the front area. I had the sense that they were very powerful men, just by the way that they were revered and respected. I realized this was a special place and these were very special men. I was brought in front of the table. They were older men eighty-five or ninety years old. I remember wondering who these entities were and what they had control over. I was not given any clues. They were the only entities I have ever seen on the other side that looked over fifty years old. They didn't look Middle Eastern, more like elders."

They "spoke without moving their lips." What they said was "beyond my comprehension." "As I stood there, one of the men in the center stood up and asked my guide, who was near my right side, 'Is this the guy you told us about?' My guide replied that it was. This leader said 'No, we do not want him at this time; he is too young and he is not ready yet.'" And that was it. Can you say what that was about? It's puzzled him all his life.

That was a council that one sees at times if someone is on a specific mission, you might say. His mission was to try to show that it's possible to be in touch with more than one realm at the same time while being a physical Earth human. And while he had come to about 35 to 38 percent positive, so to speak—had proved that much that was possible—he hadn't gone on a bit more. So I believe that he was presented because life was difficult for him then and he really would have been all right passing over right then and saying, "Okay, can this be over now?" But they said no. They were, however, his teachers and guides. He'll see them again.

Beautiful. Okay. Then he had another weird thing. He had another soul travel experience. He arrived at a "long, low building." He was standing on one side, near the middle. There were no windows—not occupied but maybe used for storage. Then he heard a lot of sounds coming from the other side of this building. "I thought I could hear someone, or maybe several people, speaking at the same time." It was a very, very, very, very long building, so he decided to kind of hop over to the other side, and he did, but there was nobody there. And then he returned to his body. What was that?

A little lesson about impatience, that's all.

Impatience, oh! [Laughs.] What should he have done?

Stay.

Oh, just stay there and somebody would come out to talk to him?

I cannot say. It didn't happen, so it was what it was.

Okay. Oh, then the next one was really strange. "After traveling very fast for what seemed a long distance . . . we came to a neighborhood that was completely strange to me. We slowly walked up the middle of a street with wooden houses on both sides . . . white in color . . . all built alike. . . . the street surface was a hard material but I didn't know what it was." It wasn't anything he was familiar with.

"This street was built on a gently sloping hill, and as I walked toward the higher end . . . I noticed that each house was a little bit higher than the previous one . . . well kept . . . I didn't see any of the inhabitants . . . they were all lived in . . . there were no driveways or garages." So this "made me think that automobiles were not used there." He doesn't know why he was shown that.

That was an ideal. Sometimes people are shown ideals, all right? I cannot say too much about that, but it was essentially an ideal. It would be as if somebody posed a question, "Would you like to live like this?" or "Would you like the world to be like this," and so on. He was being shown an ideal. One is sometimes shown such things to understand why things are the way they are—and why things are not the way they are. That's all I'm going to say about that.

Okay. "Several days later, I was escorted on the longest soul travel trip that I can remember having. There was a guide on each side of me and we traveled in an upright position as if we were walking." Usually I think he traveled, he said, prone. "The sound of passing through rushing air" and "the sensation of moving as fast as a bullet." "We were traveling a great distance. I asked my guides what they were going to do and where they were going to take me. I asked, "Who are you guys and who do you work for? Who sent you? Who's your boss—is it Jesus, Michael or who?"

"This was the first time I had ever questioned my guides or bucked up against them even a little bit. I thought surely I was not important enough for someone in high command to send two helpers out to carry out a mission. One of them told me, 'We were sent to do a job. We are not here to answer any questions or visit. Now let's go.'" And then they kind of nudged him. And where they took him was . . . "After a time, our speed of travel slowed down and instead of going in a straight line, we began to circle. I soon realized we were above a large sphere similar to our Earth. We circled completely around what I think was a planet and continued to travel in another straight line" and then "circled a second planet." They looked a lot like Earth. They were different colors, "each one letting me know there was life of some form" there. The second one was smaller. "These experiences were very intriguing, . . . but I don't know what they meant or why I was sent."

Different dimensions of Earth. That's all I'll say about that.

Different dimensions. Okay. And again, the reason they were so unfriendly was so that he wouldn't bond with them? Is that . . . ?

Always.

Okay. Oh, now this dark force! Two negative encounters: "The first time, I could tell a dark force was coming toward me. Several other spirits were around me and they started moving away. I realized a strong spirit was getting nearer and nearer, as I could feel the negativity . . . This was scary."

A moment. [Pause.] Continue reading very slowly.

There's only one more sentence: "This was . . ."

Slowly.

[Reading very slowly.] "This was scary, for it was the first time I had encountered anything except love and total acceptance while in an out-of-body situation." He quickly returned to his body, ending the experience.

Such things happen occasionally. This usually occurs when, in his case, he might have, say, been looking forward to having an encounter, and sometimes it takes a wrong turn. Keep in mind, sometimes if you take a wrong turn, you're not expected to go there at that time; you're not expected to be there at that place—things like that. Sometimes there will be an energy like that. This is, you might say, the living presence of a block. People refer to blocks: They can't do this because they're "blocked" and so on. This is the living presence of a block. He did exactly what he was supposed to do.

By quickly returning to his body?

Yes.

Okay.

For those of you who ever have experiences like that, don't hang on. Don't try and make it something that it isn't. Don't turn it into a big scenario. Just return, snap back, and come out of it right away. And always give yourself permission to do that—and by permission, I mean physical permission. So just say out loud before you do things like this or if you know you're going to have an experience like this, just say: "I give myself permission to wake up or to be conscious or to be in my body again in the most benevolent way for me now," if the experience is uncomfortable. And I use the word uncomfortable because sometimes people experience something uncomfortable and they push on. They might be determined. And occasionally, it might just be something slightly uncomfortable, like when the guides were cold. But other times, it might be: "You're not meant to go there at this time; you're not meant to go there at all." In short, it's the energy of a block. Just come out of it and wake up.

I'm trying to reach people here of different experiences. Some people might be asleep, all right? If they're asleep, it's like this: "Give yourself permission to wake up." If they're doing this as a meditation, then snap back. And when you snap back into your natural physical state, don't just sit with the energy. Move around immediately. You don't have to get up and move around—perhaps it would be better not to—but move your arms and legs, all right? Move your head around a little bit. Wiggle around in the seat. But the reason you don't just jump up and run someplace is because you may not be completely back in your body yet, and if you do that, there will be a momentary separation between your soul and your body, and your body will become frightened. You might have an anxious experience: Your heart will pound or something like that. And if you're young and strong, you'll get over that, but if you're not in the best of health, it could be a problem.

All right, now the next one—I don't have to read this if you already know what it is.

Hold on. Just pay attention. You'll know why after the session is over. Hold on for a moment again. [Pause.] I will say this one extra thing. You understand that the process going on here is a little different. You are having an intellectual experience, you understand. The channel is not. This is a full-bodied experience, so he needs extra insulation and protection, and he needs it to go slowly, okay?

Okay. [Speaks very slowly.] "The second face-to-face meeting happened"—you tell me when to stop—"a year later, and it was much more intense."

Slower.

"I found myself in the presence of a very evil force . . ."

Slower.

[Reads incredibly slowly.] ". . . much more evil than the first one. It seemed to be more than a single spirit, perhaps . . ."

Stop. Is there any more? It's important.

Yes, he followed him to the physical plane and he saw him: Six feet tall, he had hooves that were split down the middle—a monster with brown hair all over his . . .

Stop. Now I need to ask you a question. What do you know about this person? Is he Christian?

Yes. Oh, yes. Raised a Catholic. I don't know him that well, but that's what the book says.

That's all we need to know.

Okay.

This was an experience based somewhat in religious things. Sometimes people, especially youngsters, are taught—you said he was raised in the Catholic religion?

Yes. Yes, altar boy, the whole thing.

Okay, so he experienced catechism?

Yes.

Chances are, this was an experience that was an overshadowing of fear-based things. Sometimes fear-based things are taught in religion if the philosophers of that religion, meaning those who have interpreted religious documents that are not necessarily public . . . sometimes fear-based things are put in in order to protect the parishioners from taking a path that the fathers, you might say, of the religion have come to believe are not safe. So this was an experience like that, and I'd be interested to know: Did he continue on with the visions, or was that the last one?

Well, it goes quite a bit on. He's pretty brave. He stood up to it and kept saying, "God made me; God made you. He's more powerful than you are."

Don't quote it; just put it in your own words.

He stood there and stared the being down until it burst into a million dust particles.

That was well done.

Yes. But he said that even though he sold the property, when he visited there, he could never walk again in that area; he could never go back there and get close to that spot. You know that may be where the . . .

Listen. You make a note: You ask Robby to do a living-prayer cleansing of that area. I don't think that it's a serious issue for other people, but looking at the area, I can see a spot that needs to be cleared.

Okay. I made a note. You know, that may be the last experience with evil that he had—yes, that's the last one he records. So that's why it ended!

See, there's an issue. That's why I asked you. Sometimes when a person has experiences like this, they start getting too fond of the experiences, and sometimes then it's as if someone is trying to shut a door. The first time that you mentioned it, it was as if someone was trying to say, "Okay, that's enough. Time to commit to your physical life and find your happiness and joy there." And I feel . . . the reason I asked about that is I was pretty sure most people would not push on after that point. I feel that he did well in his claiming to be a child of God, and this is always good, but that he was intended to stop the experiences—actually before having that experience, on the previous one where there was that feeling, the good feeling. So pushing on that far, I feel his religious training helped him to get through that experience, but that experience itself was really not intended to happen and was definitely not associated with the previous experiences.

Okay. But it was a symbol. Yes, also in the book are meditation experiences, and that isn't really out of the body. When he held a stone that his Native American teacher had, it became hot, and later it became clear and they couldn't wake him up. [Flips through pages.] So he started going to Willy, this shaman kind of person who led meditations, and he had a meditation and they couldn't wake him up, and everybody was really scared—it was like he didn't come out of it. He doesn't know where he went or what he saw or anything— can you say anything about that?

Yes. This is not at all unusual. Especially in olden times, if he had been a member of a more ancient people, they would have just let him be, and he would have come out of it at some point. But sometimes people try to bring you up. They might try and ground you; sometimes there's even a person who comes over and grounds you. They might touch your shoulders and so on. So that's another form of it.

Now, later in Willy's class, he was told he had two animal guides: a coyote for the earth and an eagle for the air. And everybody else could see their animal guides but he couldn't see his, and it went on and on and on, and finally after a couple of more tries to see these beings, he said, "I had one of the most memorable experiences of this lifetime. When trying to see one of my animal guides, I realized I was flying above a river. I could see small objects on the ground, which I could tell were several hundred feet below me. It took me a minute or so to realize I had become a part of my eagle. I was seeing through its eyes and gliding." And he would have a feeling of flapping his wings, and the most important thing is that "this flying was a most pleasant experience and gave me the fantastic feeling of being totally free." He was the eagle; it was so fantastic. But the thing is that the next morning, his arms and his chest were so sore, he could hardly move. Everything just hurt; he was so sore for days, as if he really had been flapping his wings. Can you say anything about that?

He was doing that, to a degree. You see, because of the visions he'd been having that were real things—we're not talking about closing your eyes and doing a meditation; we're talking about the real visions you've been talking about here in this talk—he actually did that. Most people would essentially ride on the back of the eagle, but because he was used to becoming what he used to be, he became that. And that's why he was exhausted as if he'd had a tremendous workout. You know, if you suddenly go to the gymnasium and you work out and your heart and lungs are in good shape and so on, and you give yourself a tremendous workout that's much more than you probably should do—that's why they start you out slowly—that's exactly how you would feel.

His wife Jeannie had a similar experience. She saw through the horse's eyes, but she didn't become the horse.

But he did become . . .

He did. He became the eagle.

Remember to come back to this.

Come back to the eagle?

Yes, and the coyote.

Okay. And the coyote, okay. I think that's the only time. He said, "I've never had any contact with my coyote or my eagle since then."

Now, I want to give him something, then. Sometimes when you're working with shamans, they won't necessarily tell you everything about your spirit animals. Sometimes, especially if they're not sure of you as a person—how dedicated are you or how new are you to these things—they might start you out with someone. In this case, he started him out with a coyote. Partly this has to do with the fact . . . turn the machine off. [Information that followed was personal for Gene.]

We're kind of winding down here. He met a friend of his wife's, and she said, "Oh, I've seen you before! Just last week, I saw you giving a psychic lecture to a large crowd of people!" when they were both out of the body. Well, he doesn't know. He said, "I must have been on the spiritual plane having a soul-travel experience." And she also had to be out of the body, but he doesn't remember anything about it.

This is not at all unusual, and it happens much more often than people realize. And interestingly enough—and I find this interesting in humans in the passage of time—it's not a unique experience. People have been having experiences like this for thousands of years. At various times, and you're in one of those times now, it's become acceptable to say it. So it's really quite a regular experience, and even though he's only been told that on occasion, it's happened probably eighty, eighty-five times to him over the years. People have seen him doing something somewhere. They've encountered him; they saw him in their room and so on. What's not typical is to be told that.

But if you become a little more known as being a spiritual person and so on, sometimes then you are told these things. But even then, you're told maybe 2 or 3 percent of the time. Most people are shy. They don't bring that up, or they may not remember. Sometimes they'll remember years later, and it will seem like it just happened.

So he is a teacher. Does everybody teach on other planes, or is this rare? Where does he fit in with the mass of the population?

This is a teaching planet that you're on. You're all learning things to become better teachers. Many of you were teachers before you came here, and not unlike teachers that you're used to in school and so on, you continue to learn so you can teach better. So of course this is typical.

Okay, here we have Jesus. "Several days had passed . . . I was on a soul travel experience. . . I had just entered a large room through the back door. . . . The floor ran uphill toward the rear and was filled with seats. Looking around, I thought it must be a movie theater. . . . It was very light in this room and every seat was filled. There were also people standing along both walls . . . I crowded against the back wall . . . I soon realized that this huge crowd was saying something, . . . 'Jesus I love you, Jesus I love you.' . . . I soon joined in the chant.

"As I stood there chanting along with everyone else, the door on the right side of the front wall opened and Jesus walked in. The crowd became quiet and I thought that surely Jesus was going to talk to us. He looked to be thirty years old with brown hair touching his shoulders. He looked straight ahead and walked slowly, never changing his facial expression. He then turned and walked toward the middle of the room and I could only see his left profile. As he approached the center of the room, I expected him to step up on a riser or maybe just turn toward the crowd, but instead I lost sight of him. . . . I never figured out the reason I had that brief interruption in my line of sight.

"When I was able to see him again, Jesus was past the center of the room and still walking slowly. I remember thinking that he was going to leave without saying anything. Almost at that same moment, he turned to the right and continued toward the small door. . . . As time has passed and I have thought much about the experience, I think Jesus may have delivered a message and that I was not allowed to hear it. Maybe I was not ready to accept his message." Can you say something about that?

This was a combination of Earth and spirit experience, all right? So sometimes, you will see something like that and then you won't see it and then maybe it'll pick up again and you'll see it again. It's almost like focal lengths in a lens, where if the focal length is proper, you can see something, but then if it's not, if the image suddenly becomes of a different focal length, you can't see it. This is the best way I can describe it in your terms. So this was a vision meant to encourage him. No words were spoken; he was not denied the words. There were no words.

Okay. Okay, he had some questions too: "Why wasn't I allowed to hear Jesus? Why was I tested?" He was in Oklahoma and somebody saw him in California, but that's a bilocation, right?

Yes.

Ah, he asks, "How many incarnations have I lived in planet Earth," and you've already answered that. He seems to feel he had many, many, many because those psychics gave him past-life experiences.

It's important to know that there's different ways of looking at that. I am looking at what I see. What I see is that this is his first, and he's not likely to choose another.

Okay. And I don't know if you can answer this one: "Why have I been unable to see my late wife Jeannie," who was his soul mate, "and my son Chris since they died? I've seen my grandmother, my grandfather . . ."

I can't answer questions like this through another person. These are very personal. You are asking it as a question. He would say it with feeling. It's not the same when somebody else asks. He is not meant to see these things, okay? Tell him he will see them all when the time is right.

Oh, I left out the most important one, the biggest one! He went through the tunnel of light, and there were beings on the other side, and he never felt such love. It was like a near-death experience, such powerful love. But he knew if he took one step into the light—they were inviting him to come farther—that he wouldn't be able to go back, and he had young children. But for the rest of his life, he knew there was life after death. He knew there was love. His life changed. Can you just say a little bit about that, why he had that experience?

It was just to remind him of the continuity of love. Good night.

Thank you very, very much. Thank you.

CHAPTER THIRTY-FOUR

How You Traverse to Your Home Planet in Deep Sleep to Recharge

Soul Portal through Robert Shapiro

2 FEBRUARY 2010

Greetings.

Greetings!

I have not done this before, so there may be a few pauses because I am functioning.

That's wonderful. Whatever it takes.

We Support Your Nightly Passage to Your Home Planets

I work as an intermediary between worlds. There are many of us in existence—millions, many millions. We are part of the living spirit world that must be close to you all, all the time, in order to keep your world stable and to allow for your comings and goings. All of you on the soul level are from other planets, and you are not at home on Earth. As a result, you must go to your other planets in your deep-sleep state and recharge your existence. Beings like myself will connect to anywhere from thirty or forty individuals—and sometimes some groups of individuals up to a hundred, sometimes even more—to act as intermediaries to support moments of passage of your unconscious sleeping self to your home planets in this universe or beyond. This is why there are so many of us here.

We do not originate on this planet, but we have the capability to be present on your planet without any adaptation or training. We seem to be some of the few who can do this, and we are not here for anyone other than the human being. This allows you as individuals to traverse, then, perhaps three or four times in a twenty-four-hour day, often happening in between teachings with your guides, teachers, angels, and so on. At the deep-sleep state, you might go temporarily to your home planet, but what you do there is not what you might think.

You may not know that this is necessary, but what you do there more than anything else is that, as a soul being, you will go to your home planet, and even though you are not physical there—you might even appear like a spot of light—occasionally you might appear in the form of life associated with that planet that you identify with. Almost the first thing you do is breathe. By "breathe," I do not mean take in air as you do here on Earth, but rather you will take in the energy of that place, just a deep reception that I would call breathing, but you do not exhale anything from Earth.

The reason this happens is that we are connected there, meaning we have the capacity to function as an intermediary, which is like a living portal creating a truly conscious portal, by which you can make such a journey instantaneously so that all other beings are insulated and protected from all that you are on Earth that may be uncomfortable to them, including the planets. Anything on the home planet that may be incompatible with your soul does not affect you or cause any detrimental or otherwise influence to affect your life on Earth.

I personally have been functioning in this capacity on your planet now for about a thousand years. As we get more experienced and have been here longer, some of us grow larger. When we are newly arrived, some of us are smaller, but this is not a fixed situation. Sometimes [chuckles] some stay small no matter how experienced they are. But we are not assigned, you see, to souls, so we might have thousands of experiences with different souls, many experiences with some souls or anything in between.

Generally speaking, the dots that seem to make up our being have to do with one or more traverses, so what you're really seeing is something that's a tube. If you were to see a tube in a cross-section, it would look very much like a circle. So that's what you're really seeing. It isn't a plasma that makes us up. If you were to see us in our natural state, we usually would appear as a single color and there would be none of this "little circles" stuff [chuckles]. I'm getting used to your language here.

Your Souls Have the Same Shape We Do

So I cannot tell you where I am from, because, as I have been told, it's vitally important that this remain a secret to you. I can say that it's at the outer boundaries of this universe, but that's all I can say. This may be why we are able to help Earth souls traverse to a home planet beyond this universe, because we are used to being in our state at home. We are used to being at the border of things. Perhaps this is why we can function in an unusual capacity this way. Generally speaking, we do not stay in this capacity for more than a thousand years. I have lingered a bit and I might linger for a couple more years, but soon I will return to my home place. We are not humanoids, as is obvious, but we do have lives. We also do not have a fixed amount of life but exist in an ongoing fashion.

Which we would call immortal, right?

Yes, but this is what you are too when you are not in your adventurous mode exploring different life forms. You do not look exactly like us, but on examination, you would be circular in form. This is why perhaps we were requested to come, because your souls have the same shape that we do. When you are at the deep-sleep state, you are most at ease with beings who are circular like yourselves. In this way, there is a natural, built-in compatibility.

What do we do when we get there? Just take in the energy?

You do the same thing, yes, with the energy. It's like if you've ever taken a deep breath of fresh air and felt that sense of exhilaration and refreshment. It's very much like that experience, which is part of the reason why a person can have a nap for twenty or thirty minutes and wake up profoundly refreshed, whereas they might sleep for four or five hours and not really have that experience.

So it means you went home during that time?

That's what it always means.

Our Different Colors Accommodate the Soul's Different Feelings

I saw the picture of you that was taken close to Bradshaw Ranch and you had many, many, many colors in these little tiny circles. Are you saying that each one of these represents a traverse for souls?

Yes. The reason there are different colors is that it accommodates the soul's different moods. When the soul is coming from Earth, traversing wherever it needs to go, it will still have feelings. Even at the deep-sleep level, there are strong feelings. The colors accommodate those feelings, both going to the home planet and returning, so that when you are, say, passing through Earth, you leave those feelings, and by the time you get to the home planet, you are in a state of being in which you can be totally receptive. But when you return, you must pick up at least a portion of those feelings so that you are reminded who you are and can return at ease without resistance to your physical self. Otherwise, you would not want to go back to your physical self.

So the colors have to do with feelings. We do not feel these feelings, although they are within the tubes as you might see them within us. Thus we are insulated from feeling the feelings, but with some photographs of you I've seen that are taken here and there over the world, you can see the energy feeling. Different colors are not always associated with the same feelings. It depends largely on the individual or their family of souls. Some groups of souls will radiate this or that color for the same feeling, and other groups of souls might have an identical feeling and radiate a different color. So there's much variety, I have noted.

Do the humans in deep sleep go to you, or do you go to them? How do you connect with them?

It is not a problem of time or space. Wherever I am and wherever they are is not a difficulty. Once you are in the deep-sleep state and your soul can traverse, there is no limit to where you could be. I could be inside a mountain—just as an example, though I don't do that—and you could easily come and make your passage.

Okay, but do we go to you? Do the same souls always go to the same beings like you?

Oh yes, you would come. You would have to come in order to make a safe transit.

So we come to you?

Yes.

Do we always go to the same being?

I do not know that. It is possible that you might have more than one.

So when you first came here a thousand years ago—that would be AD 1000—how much did you see of Earth?

Not very much. In order to perform such a function, I need to have a strong connection to my home planet so that I do not lose myself, my personality, with such passages. So I do not really observe your history, your culture or anything like that. To the degree I know you, it is in my relationship with your souls. It is not based on your experience on the Earth. My relationship, then, is that I feel you with your essential mood as you make your traverse through and then into your home zone, so to speak. When you come back, you are a bit more comfortable for me because you are completely clear, but then you traverse back and I am releasing some of that matter of your feelings, as I said before. So I do not observe your history and manners and mores and all that.

I Am Stabilizing Your Energy

How did you happen to come here? Did someone go to your home planet and request that you do this for the humans on Earth?

That's how all of us have volunteered to do this, because we were requested to come here to create a much better stabilized energy. When the first humans were on the Earth—not really your people—it wasn't necessary, because Earth in those times was benevolent. But once the Explorer Race, as you are deemed, came and there was some discomfiture, there needed to be not only a means to stabilize your traversing to your home planets, as I've mentioned, but also a means to insulate the planet and the planet's other life forms from such jolts, you might say, to the veil system that protects your planet and protects other planets from what happens on this place, on Earth.

So we were asked to come in as great a number as needed. That's why I say there are millions of us, but one can perform such services for many souls. Even though you might have billions of individuals, millions of us are enough.

What was your life like before you came here?

Oh, very calm: a benign and benevolent existence with communication of ideas and concepts, like that. I wouldn't say we were purely intellectual, but that was part of our pursuits.

Do you have a form there?

We look the same here with the exception that you do not see all the little circles. We are of one color, but we would be circular.

Ah! So before you come and then also after you go back home, all the circles are gone?

Yes, because the circles . . .

Are the portals.

That's right, the traversing mechanism. It is not part of our physical functionality. Some have said it is a kind of plasma that makes us up, and as well-intended an analysis as that is, that is not the case. In our natural state, we would just be circular, with no "tubes." I'm using that as a simplified means by which you can imagine in your mind's eye what that might look like, because you are familiar with tubes.

You said you keep a strong connection to your home planet. So then are you able to connect with the rest of the beings there while you're doing this, or do you have to not do that because of the discomfort?

Usually I would do that—speaking for myself—when traversing is not going on. I cannot have traversing going on for a few time segments and then connect to my home planet to refresh myself. For you, such a refreshment would come in sleep. For me, it is more of being present there, during which time I do something not unlike what you do. I take it in. But I don't exhale in that sense.

You take in the energy of your home planet?

That's right, and this refreshes me.

And gives you the strength to keep doing this?

Strength is not actually a factor. We have a natural endurance.

This is amazing. We knew we had to go somewhere during sleep to get recharged, but no one ever said before how the process worked.

This is my experience of it. I do not claim to have all knowledge, but I'm sharing what I know based on my experience.

Well, I'm sure that the others of your kind do something similar.

The Service Is the Joy

Are there any special joys in doing this? I mean, do you get satisfaction from it or is it just a service?

The service is the joy. To be of service is a great pleasure. You on your planet know this pleasure, because you might do little things throughout the day where you are in service to others, and often there is pleasure associated with that. There might be other times perhaps for you when it is a burden, but it is not a burden for me or the others of my fellow beings, as far as I know, because what we do is one thing. If there were a multitude of things we had to do at the same time, then that might be too much. But the function we provide is something we can do and is easy for us, and therefore, it is a joy of service situation, as you yourself mentioned.

To be of service is natural for all forms of life. Even though there are extremes on your own planet, such as beings consuming each other, still that's a service. From my understanding of your planet—not based on day-to-day observation but simply on what has been explained to us before we came here for service—the whole interaction of all beings on your planet is largely service. So this is part of your nature as well.

The reason you can do this, you said, is that you're from the edge of the universe. You exist at the borders, so in your natural state, do you go to other universes—when you're home?

First off, I think you've made a slight error in your question if you're saying the reason we can do this is because we are at the edge of the universe. In fact, there are many other forms of life at or around the same "edge," and they do not do it. The reason we do it, can do it, is because of our makeup, because of who we are. I believe the reason we are able to more easily accommodate such an action is because of our location, but I cannot state with certainty that this is so. It is what I have come to believe. But I do not claim to have, as I say, all answers. So you can perhaps rephrase the question?

You Are Taking Service to Another Level

You said you could do this because of your makeup, because of who you are. Can you say a little more about that?

Not too much, but we are what you are when you're not performing such a service, as is all life in this universe. And we do not have any need to forget who we are. It's important to note that so you do not put a distance between yourselves and us.

Well, you know, the Explorer Race has some great goals. What do you think about the concept?

It is very advanced, taking service to another level—being of service to the entire universe at the very least.

Hopefully, all universes.

Yet there are profound risks involved. I can see that it is essential to keep it all very well bundled so it doesn't affect other planets, the rest of the universe, and so on. So it's too soon for me to say that I think it's a good thing or I think it needs more thought. Ask me that question again when you have completed your service here.

Okay. Why a thousand years? Who picked that as your length of service here?

Nobody did. It's just what I have chosen.

Oh! It's different for all of your beings?

Yes, it's entirely associated with the individual. Some, I think, have been here for close to 3,000 years. But with me, I think I would like to return to my home planet soon.

What do you look forward to there?

The exchange of ideas and the interactions from one to another. Nothing complicated. It is essentially summed up by saying a single word: "home." I think we will have to stop this session soon.

You've given us incredible information that helps us understand how our lives are possible here.

I believe, on your world, with you as souls in human form, that you are constantly surrounded in every waking and sleeping moment with a vast fabric of spirit and other physical forms that make it possible for you to continue the delicate balance of your lives on Earth. From what I have been guided before coming to this place, it is a very delicate balance indeed. Yet from the angelic messenger from Creator who came initially to explain why and what and so on about your service on Earth as souls, I believe that your intention is of the highest and I wish you well in your pathway to accomplish such a worthy goal. Good night.

Thank you very much. Good life.

TIME AND THE TRANSITION TO NATURAL TIME

through Robert Shaprio

"The purpose of this book is to provide a context for your lives in the sequence you find yourselves in now. This explanation of time—and, to a degree, its variables—is being provided for you so that you will understand more about your true, natural, native personalities and so that you will be reminded that you are, as you know, in a school and that this school is purely temporary.

You don't come here very often to this place of linear time; like your own human lives, you are in school for only so long, and then you live your lives. When you exist beyond this school, you will find all those lives infinitely easier. And even as the Creator, your lives will be easier than they are in their single, linear existences you're living now, because you will have all your components."

—Founder of Time

$16.95

ISBN 978-1-891824-85-2
Softcover, 286 PP.

Chapters Include:

- Time Is Now Available for Your Personal Flexibility
- You Live in a Stream Hosted by Planet Earth
- Moving Toward Complete Safety and Benevolence
- The Gift of Time
- You Are Here to Learn About Your Personal Physicality
- Letting Go of Conflict in the Next Focus
- Your Blinders Are Coming Off
- Time Is an Application for Expansion
- Transition to the Future in Warmth and Safety
- Linking from Future Selves
- Making the Transition through Deep Sleep
- There Are Many Expressions of Time

THE ANCIENT SECRET OF THE FLOWER OF LIFE
VOLUME 1
by Drunvalo Malchizedek

Once, all life in the universe knew the Flower of Life as the creation pattern—the geometrical design leading us into and out of physical existence. Then, from a very high state of consciousness, we fell into darkness, the secret hidden for thousands of years, encoded in the cells of all life.

Now we are rising from the darkness and a new dawn is streaming through the windows of perception. This book is one of those windows. Drunvalo Melchizedek presents in text and graphics the Flower of Life Workshop, illuminating the mysteries of how we came to be.

Sacred Geometry is the form beneath our being and points to a divine order in our reality. We can follow that order from the invisible atom to the infinite stars, finding ourselves at each step. The information here is one path, but between the lines and drawings lie the feminine gems of intuitive understanding. You might see them sparkle around some of these provocative ideas:

- Remembering Our Ancient Past
- The Secret of the Flower Unfolds
- The Darker Side of Our Present and Past
- The Geometries of the Human Body
- When Evolution Crashed, and the Christ Grid Arose
- Egypt's Role in the Evolution of Consciousness
- The Significance of Shape and Structure

$25.00 Softcover 228 P.

ISBN 1-891824-17-1

Available from your favorite bookstore or:

LIGHT TECHNOLOGY PUBLISHING
PO Box 3540 • Flagstaff, AZ 86003

Drunvalo Melchizedek's life experience reads like an encyclopedia of breakthroughs in human endeavor. He studied physics and art at the University of California at Berkeley, but he feels that his most important education came after college. In the past 25 years, he has studied with over 70 teachers from all belief systems and religious understandings.

For some time now, he has been bringing his vision to the world through the Flower of Life program and the Mer-Ka-Ba meditation. This teaching encompasses every area of human understanding, explores the development of humankind from ancient civilizations to the present time and offers clarity regarding the world's state of consciousness and what is needed for a smooth and easy transition into the 21st century.

THE ANCIENT SECRET OF THE FLOWER OF LIFE
VOLUME 2

$25.00 Softcover 252 P.
ISBN 1-891824-21-X

- The Unfolding of the Third Informational System
- Whispers from Our Ancient Heritage
- Unveiling the Mer-ka-ba Meditation
- Using Your Mer-ka-ba
- Connecting to the Levels of Self
- Two Cosmic Experiments
- What We May Expect in the Forthcoming Dimensional Shift

The sacred Flower of Life pattern, the primary geometric generator of all physical form, is explored in even more depth in this volume, the second half of the famed Flower of Life workshop. The proportions of the human body, the nuances of human consciousness, the sizes and distances of the stars, planets and moons, even the creations of humankind, are all shown to reflect their origins in this beautiful and divine image. Through an intricate and detailed geometrical mapping, Drunvalo Melchizedek shows how the seemingly simple design of the Flower of Life contains the genesis of our entire third-dimensional existence.

From the pyramids and mysteries of Egypt to the new race of Indigo children, Drunvalo presents the sacred geometries of the Reality and the subtle energies that shape our world. We are led through a divinely inspired labyrinth of science and stories, logic and coincidence, on a path of remembering where we come from and the wonder and magic of who we are.

Finally, for the first time in print, Drunvalo shares the instructions for the Mer-Ka-Ba meditation, step-by-step techniques for the re-creation of the energy field of the evolved human, which is the key to ascension and the next dimensional world. If done from love, this ancient process of breathing prana opens up for us a world of tantalizing possibility in this dimension, from protective powers to the healing of oneself, of others and even of the planet.

Available from your favorite bookstore or:

LIGHT TECHNOLOGY PUBLISHING
PO Box 3540 • Flagstaff, AZ 86003

Phone: 928-526-1345 or 1-800-450-0985 • Fax: 923-714-1132

SEDONA Journal of EMERGENCE!

ORDER NOW! TO RECEIVE SPECTACULAR SAVINGS!

ORDER ONLINE!
SAVE expensive freight or postage on your Sedona Journal subscription

We are now making ELECTRONIC SUBSCRIPTIONS available for the SEDONA JOURNAL OF EMERGENCE!

We have now added content that will not fit into the printed magazine!

- Get the entire Journal online by subscription—and get it 2 weeks before it goes on the newstand!
- Save on expensive freight or postage on your Sedona Journal subscription!

Electronic Subscriptions

❒ 1 yr. . . . .$29 ❒ 2 yr. $55

All Electronic and Combo Subscriptions *MUST* be purchased online at: www.sedonajournal.com to obtain username and password

Get the Best of Both Worlds! Special Combo Offers!

U.S.A

Get a Printed Subscription Along with an Electronic Subscription - U.S.A. only

1st Class ❒ 1 yr. . . $82 ❒ 2 yr. . . $159
2nd Class ❒ 1 yr. . . $59 ❒ 2 yr. . . $109

Canada & Mexico

Get an Airmail Printed Subscription Along with an Electronic Subscription for only

❒ 1 yr. . . . $95 ❒ 2 yr. . . . $179

NOTE: The U.S. Postal Service has changed postal rates, eliminating Canadian 2nd Class Surface and increasing all airmail rates.

All Countries
Except U.S.A., Canada, & Mexico

Get an Airmail Printed Subscription Along with an Electronic Subscription for only

❒ 1 yr. . . . $152 ❒ 2 yr. . . . $285

NOTE: The U.S. Postal Service has changed postal rates, eliminating global 2nd Class Surface and increasing all airmail rates.

yes! Send Me:

Printed and Mailed Subcriptions

USA

1st Class	2nd Class
❒ 2 yrs. $129	❒ 2 yrs. $79
❒ 1 yr. $65	❒ 1 yr. $43

CANADA & MEXICO

AIR
❒ 2 yrs (24 issues) $149
❒ 1 yr (12 issues). $79
U.S. dollars only

NOTE: The US Postal Service has changed postal rates, eliminating Canadian 2nd Class Surface and increasing all airmail rates.

ALL COUNTRIES Except USA, Canada & Mexico

AIR
❒ 2 yrs (24 issues) $255
❒ 1 yr (12 issues). $136
U.S. dollars only

NOTE: The US Postal Service has changed postal rates, eliminating global 2nd Class Surface and increasing all airmail rates.

My Name ____________________
Address ____________________
City ____________________ State: ______
Zip: ____________________ Phone ______
Email ____________________
Gift Recipient Name ____________________
Address ____________________
City ____________________ State: ______
Zip: ____________________
Personalized Gift Card from ____________________

METHOD OF PAYMENT:

❒ CHECK # ❒ M.O.
❒ VISA ❒ MASTERCARD ❒ NOVUS ❒ AMEX

CARD NO. ____________________
EXPIRATION DATE ____________________
SIGNATURE ____________________